The Pictorial Treasury of Film Stars

SPENCER TRACY

**by
ROMANO TOZZI**

General Editor: **TED SENNETT**

GALAHAD BOOKS · NEW YORK CITY

To my Mother and Father

Library of Congress Catalog Card Number: 74-33234
ISBN: 0-88365-289-7

Published by arrangement with Pyramid Communications, Inc.

Manufactured in the United States of America

PREFACE

By TED SENNETT

"The movies!" Flickering lights in the darkness that stirred our imaginations and haunted our dreams. All of us cherish memories of "going to the movies" to gasp at feats of derring-do, to roar with laughter at clownish antics, to weep at acts of noble sacrifice. For many filmgoers, the events on the screen were not only larger than life but also more mysterious, more fascinating, and—when times were bad—more rewarding. And if audiences could be blamed for preferring movies to life, they never seemed to notice, or care.

Of course the movies have always been more than a source of wish-fulfillment or a repository for nostalgic memories. From the first unsteady images to today's most experimental efforts, motion pictures have mirrored America's social history, and over the decades they have developed into an internationally esteemed art.

As social history, movies reflect our changing tastes, styles, and ideas. To our amusement, they show us how we looked and behaved: flappers with bobbed hair and bee-stung lips cavorting at "wild" parties; gangsters and G-men in striped suits and wide-brimmed hats exchanging gunfire in city streets; pompadoured "swing-shift" Susies and dashing servicemen, "working for Uncle Sam." To our chagrin, they show us the innocent (and sometimes not so innocent) lies we believed: that love triumphs over all adversity and even comes to broad-shouldered lady executives; that war is an heroic and virtually bloodless activity; that fame and success can be achieved indiscriminately by chorus girls, scientists, football players, and artists. To our edification, they show us how we felt about marriage in the twenties, crime in the thirties, war in the forties, big business in the fifties, and youth in the sixties. (Presumably future filmgoers will know how we felt about sex in the seventies.)

As an influential art, motion pictures are being studied and analyzed as never before by young filmgoers who are excited by the medium's past accomplishments and its even greater potential for the future. The rich body of films from *Intolerance* to *The Godfather;* the work of directors from Griffith to Kubrick; the uses of film for documenting events, ideas, and even emotions—these are the abundant materials from which film courses and film societies are being created across the country.

THE PICTORIAL TREASURY OF FILM STARS also draws on these materials, encompassing in a series of publications all the people, the trends, and the concepts that have contributed to motion pictures as nostalgia, as social history, and as art. The books in the series range as widely as the camera-eye can take us, from the distant past when artists with a vision of film's possibilities shaped a new form of expression, to the immediate future, when the medium may well undergo changes as innovative as the first primitive movements.

THE PICTORIAL TREASURY OF FILM STARS is a tribute to achievement: to the charismatic stars who linger in all our memories, and to the gifted people behind the cameras: the directors, the producers, the writers, the editors, the cameramen. It is also a salute to everyone who loves movies, forgives their failures, and acknowledges their shortcomings, who attends Bogart and Marx Brothers revivals and Ingmar Bergman retrospectives and festivals of forthcoming American and European films.

"The movies!" The cameras turn and the flickering images begin. And again we settle back to watch the screen, hoping to see a dream made real, an idea made palpable, or a promise fulfilled. On that unquenchable hope alone, the movies will endure.

ACKNOWLEDGMENTS

George Caudill, Richard Crane; Lincoln Center Reference Department of the New York Library; Ted Sennett; Charles Silver of the Museum of Modern Art; Ralph Straughn. Special thanks to Wally Dauler of Audio-Brandon Films for arranging the screening of key films.

Photographs: Jerry Vermilye, Movie Star News

CONTENTS

Spencer Tracy had a rare quality of naturalness and a gift for underplaying that made him seem to *be* the person he was enacting on the screen. Audiences could identify with him, with his rugged Irish face, his straightforward manner, his warmth and earthiness. He had the ability to get inside his characters and bring them vividly to life. He could vitalize an inferior script by the sheer force of his personality. This dynamic extra dimension is hard to define. Comparatively few actors have it. But, like Tracy, they can charge a scene with such intensity that it becomes a memorable experience to watch it.

Tracy often deprecated the art of acting. He said he really didn't like his work, but that it required little effort on his part and enabled him to achieve financial security. The people associated with him throughout his long career knew otherwise—and so did he. His profession did make him a wealthy man, but only after years of hard work and much personal suffering. He was a perfectionist and a constant worrier who poured an enormous amount of concentration, study, and effort into the preparation of each new role. His standards were high and he had great integrity. He always wanted to

INTRODUCTION

give his best, and it was difficult for him to compromise when he found himself involved in films he considered worthless or wrong for him. He was not always the best judge of vehicles and frequently turned down good parts in favor of films that did nothing to enhance his reputation.

During the thirties, frustration over his work as well as his own complex nature led to heavy drinking, open rebellion, and erratic behavior. In later years, he acquired emotional stability and sufficient perspective to cope with his problems. Although he was never an easy man to understand or get along with, he evolved an unorthodox life-style that worked for him. With the help of an understanding family and devoted friends, he achieved peace of mind and a personal happiness and professional satisfaction he hadn't known before. The early days may have taken their toll and contributed to the eventual breakdown of his health, but Spencer Tracy did come to grips with himself.

In one of his lesser films, *The People Against O'Hara*, Tracy spoke prophetic words: "It doesn't matter how long a man lives; it's how well he lives." Spencer Tracy led a rich, full life.

Spencer Tracy's many distinguished performances established him as one of the screen's most popular and durable actors. His acting range may not have been as wide as some of his contemporaries, but he was always superb when he remained within that range. He excelled in both rugged, realistic roles and in parts that called for warmth, wisdom, and humanity. He had a profound knowledge of people and a keen sense of humor that made comedy seem as effortless for him as drama.

Tracy's work continues to influence actors and stir audiences. His legacy to the world is contained in his best films. Despite his modesty and his crankiness, it is a legacy he would be proud to acknowledge.

Spencer Bonaventure Tracy was born in Milwaukee, Wisconsin, on April 5, 1900. His father, John Edward Tracy, general sales manager of the Sterling Motor Truck Company, was a staunch "God-fearing" Irishman and a devout Catholic. Spencer's mother, Carrie Brown Tracy, came from solid midwestern stock. Her family could trace its ancestors back to the early Massachusetts colonists. There was an older brother, Carroll, born in 1896.

The Tracys lived on Prospect Avenue in a comfortable house of their own. But young Spencer was drawn to a nearby district called Tory Hill, where kids had to be tough to survive. In this environment, he spent a turbulent childhood, fighting and constantly getting into scraps with other boys. Although bright and aggressive, the copper-haired, blue-eyed youngster was hard to manage. When he was seven, he ran away from home because he hated school. It happened more than once, and he was expelled from no less than fifteen grade schools before he finally received a diploma from St. Rosa's Parochial School.

During these formative years, Spencer became an avid "moving-picture" fan. He passed many happy hours at the local

BOYHOOD, ADOLESCENCE, AND EARLY MANHOOD

nickelodeons. Tracy once told writer J. P. McEvoy that he would never have gone to school at all "if there had been any other way of learning to read the titles in the silent movies."

Actor Pat O'Brien (real name: William Joseph O'Brien) was a boyhood friend of Tracy's, who studied at Marquette Academy, a Jesuit high school. One day, sixteen-year-old Spencer surprised his family by asking to be sent there. At Marquette, he developed into a better-than-average student. A new interest in theology may have been the reason. For a time he considered entering the priesthood, a vocation that would have won his father's approval.

The outbreak of World War I changed his mind. Caught up in the patriotic fervor, Spencer tried to join the Marine Corps, but he was too young. Bill O'Brien enlisted in the Navy, and told Spencer he could do the same with his parents' consent. The Tracys agreed, but only if Spencer would promise to graduate from high school when he returned.

Following basic training at Chicago's Great Lakes Naval Training Center and a seven-month tour of duty at Norfolk Navy Yard, Spencer returned to Marquette Academy to keep his promise to his parents and to find a direction for his life. Finally, after attending Northwestern Military and Naval Academy at Lake Geneva, Wisconsin, Tracy graduated from high school.

Around this time, Spencer began to think about acting as a possible career. (It was an ambition shared by Bill O'Brien.) He knew his parents would never approve—his father had hoped Spencer would join him in the trucking business. Once again he surprised his family by announcing that he intended to go to college. He told them that he wanted to become a doctor. Spencer was admitted to Milwaukee's Ripon College in January 1921.

J. Clark Graham, head of Ripon's dramatic society, liked young Tracy's forceful speaking voice. Graham encouraged him to try out for a leading role in a school production of Clyde Fitch's *The Truth*. Spencer won the part and was so successful in it that he became the talk of the campus.

At Ripon, Spencer also appeared in *The Valiant,* a one-act play. According to local reports

at the time, Tracy portrayed a condemned convict with surprising power and conviction. This second personal triumph was witnessed by his proud parents who came to see a performance. But they were concerned when he informed them that he might pursue a career in the theater before graduating from college.

During Tracy's second year at Ripon, he joined the three-man debating team under the supervision of H. P. Boody, another Ripon professor. The team embarked on an extensive intercollegiate tour that included not only the midwestern and eastern United States, but also Canada. There would be a three-day stopover in New York City. Professor Graham, aware that Tracy was planning to give up college for the stage, advised him to apply for admission at the American Academy of Dramatic Arts in New York. The AADA was considered the finest training school for actors in the country. Graham wrote a letter of recommendation, which resulted in an invitation for Tracy to audition.

In March 1922, Tracy arrived in New York, kept his appointment with the academy, and was accepted as a student. After Spencer completed the debating tour, he left college and went to visit his family. Although

John Tracy disapproved of his son's decision, he agreed to pay Spencer's tuition at the AADA if he could live on the thirty-dollar-a-month allowance provided by the government to veterans who continued their studies at an approved school.

The following month (April 1922), Spencer Tracy began classes at the AADA. Bill O'Brien, who had given up the study of law, was already enrolled there. The two young actors were launched in their acting careers.

Tracy and O'Brien took a room together in a West Side boarding house near Ninety-eighth Street. Much of the time they existed on "rice, pretzels and water."

At the academy, Tracy had one distinct advantage—an exceptional ability to memorize long speeches quickly. He developed this gift at Ripon and made use of it throughout his career. Charles Jehlinger, a teacher at the academy, was impressed with Spencer's progress. Jehlinger said years later: "If Tracy understood you—and he did almost always —he did what you asked of him immediately and decisively. He was a most responsive pupil."

During their first year at the AADA, O'Brien dropped out and took a job, but Tracy hung on. When not attending classes, he made the rounds of the casting offices. A fellow student, Monroe Owsley, tipped him off that the Theatre Guild required a large cast for its production of Karel Capek's expressionistic drama R.U.R. Tracy was able to get a nonspeaking bit as a robot. The salary: fifteen dollars a week. More robots were needed, so O'Brien joined the cast. R.U.R. opened at the Garrick Theater on October 9, 1922, for a respectable run of 184 performances. During that time, Tracy took over a one-line part and his sala-

THE STRUGGLING YOUNG STAGE ACTOR

ry was raised to twenty-five dollars.

Tracy graduated from the AADA in the spring of 1923. Graduation ceremonies included a production of Oscar Wilde's *The Importance of Being Earnest,* and also a presentation of short plays and scenes that took place at the Lyceum Theater in Manhattan. Tracy received warm praise for his efforts in the program but although theatrical agents were present, no offers were forthcoming. His monthly allowance ended with graduation.

The next weeks were difficult. *R.U.R.* closed and Tracy could not find another job. He got nowhere at the casting offices. When his money ran out, he was ready to give up and go back to Milwaukee. At this bleak moment, Tracy received a call from Leonard Woods, Jr., whose stock company was appearing in White Plains. He needed an actor for a few speaking roles, and Tracy accepted readily.

Louise Treadwell, a young actress with one Broadway credit, had also been engaged by

Woods. She and Tracy took the same train to White Plains. They met at the station and agreed to share a taxi to the theater. Recently, Louise reminisced about that first encounter. "I found him a most attractive man from the very moment I met him. Such a strong face, such a marvelous sense of humor."

Tracy played two small roles in *The Man Who Came Back*, his first play with Woods. He delivered one line—"to hell with him"—with such impact that audiences responded with applause.

Louise Treadwell and Tracy fell in love during those first hectic weeks in White Plains, performing one play in the evening and rehearsing another the next day. In June 1923, a month after their meeting, they became engaged. By that time, the Woods company had moved to Fall River, Massachusetts, where Tracy and Louise appeared in the old knockabout farce *Getting Gertie's Garter*, among others. Spencer's first stock engagement ended in Lancaster, Pennsylvania, but he and Louise found work with another company in Cincinnati. They were married in that city on September 12, 1923.

Through an agent, Tracy got a chance to return to New York for an audition with producer Arthur Hopkins. This led to his first real part on Broadway —a small role in Zoe Akins's comedy *A Royal Fandango*, starring Ethel Barrymore. The cast included Edward G. Robinson. The two actors became lifelong friends, but never worked together again. *A Royal Fandango* opened at the Plymouth Theater on November 12, 1923, to disastrous reviews. Only Miss Barrymore's personal following kept it alive for twenty-four performances. She was kind to Tracy, and introduced him to her brother Lionel, an actor he admired greatly.

Before the end of the year, Louise was expecting a baby. This created serious financial problems. Tracy's parents invited his wife to live with them while he took whatever stock job came his way. During 1924, there were engagements in Canada, New Jersey, Ohio, and Pennsylvania. Tracy managed a few days off from William Wright's company in Grand Rapids, Michigan, to be in Milwaukee for the birth of his son John on June 26, 1924.

In Grand Rapids, the Wright company tried out a new play called *Page the Duke* in which Tracy had a good role. Earle Boothe, a New York theatrical manager, went to see if it was suitable for Broadway. It wasn't, but Tracy's personality and acting ability caught Boothe's eye. He offered Tracy a prominent role in *The Sheepman,* a play intended for Broadway. It got no further than Stamford, Connecticut.

Throughout this frustrating period, Tracy's chief source of encouragement was his wife. Without her moral support and firm belief in his talent, he probably would have quit. In later years, he always gave her credit for his ultimate success.

The first tragedy in Tracy's life was the discovery of his son's deafness, a few months after the baby's birth. He sought relief in heavy drinking from guilt feelings that John's affliction was due to some genetic effect he had passed on. When doctors assured Tracy that he was wrong, he was determined more than ever to succeed in order to obtain the best possible medical care for the child.

Tracy continued the backbreaking grind of short engagements and one-night stands on the road—in winter and summer stock. He rejoined William Wright's troupe and, in late 1925, signed with Frank McCoy to be leading actor of a resident company in Trenton, New Jersey. By this time, he had appeared in over fifty plays without achieving recognition.

Selena Royle, a young actress who had worked with Tracy in stock, provided some hope. She was in New York rehearsing in *Yellow,* a new melodrama which George M. Cohan was producing. A key supporting role was still available and Miss Royle had persuaded Cohan to let Tracy read for it. He went to New York, met Cohan, and won the part. During rehearsals, the veteran actor - playwright - producer told Tracy he was the "best damned actor" he had ever seen. (His only advice to Tracy: "Act less and listen to the other actors." Tracy quoted it for years afterward.)

Margaret Vernon's play about a callous heel (Chester Morris) and his betrayed girlfriend (Shirley Warde) opened at the National Theater on September 21, 1926. Reviews were mixed, but because of its excellent acting it achieved a Broadway run of one hundred thirty-five performances. Cohan was so pleased with Tracy that he promised him a good part in a comedy that he himself was writing. When *Yellow* closed in 1927, he kept his word. His farce, *The Baby Cyclone,* contained a choice part tailored to Tracy's talents.

The play opened at Henry Miller's Theater on September 12, 1927. It was a hit. The cast included Grant Mitchell, Nan Sunderland, and Natalie Moorhead. Tracy almost stole the show in this entertaining bit of nonsense involving two couples who fight over a Pekinese. One reviewer wrote: "Spencer Tracy does the outstanding work of the evening, making the role of a long-suffering husband, who longs to sock his wife, both amusing as farce and credible as characterization."

The Baby Cyclone established Tracy as a promising Broadway newcomer. Not wishing to be typed as a comedian, he began looking for roles that offered some dramatic scope. In 1928, he accepted an important part in a road-company production of Sidney Howard's *Ned McCobb's Daughter*. Tracy benefited from the experience, under John Cromwell's direction.

Back in New York, Tracy found no new role waiting for him. Cohan came to the rescue by putting him into the touring company of *Whispering Friends*, which had just completed its Broadway run. Tracy took over the part created by William Harrigan. This comedy was another "much-ado-about-nothing" concerning two quarreling couples.

During this time, Tracy suffered a second tragic event—his father's death from cancer. Spencer believed that the elder Tracy was at last beginning to appreciate his son's abilities as an actor. Spencer had barely become adjusted to his own son's condition. And now the loss of his father had an equally devastating effect. But he tried to keep working despite his depressed state of mind.

There were opportunities to appear in several Broadway plays. Either he decided they were not right for him or he fought with directors. Finally he was forced to return to stock. Bill (now Pat) O'Brien, who had been making some progress in the theater, got a Baltimore Christmas booking for Tracy and himself. They were together in a play called *Tenth Avenue*. It was their first joint appearance.

Nineteen-twenty-nine was a busy year for Spencer Tracy— and a disconcerting one. He was seen in three Broadway failures and another that only got as far as Brooklyn. The first, *Conflict*, gave him his most challenging assignment to date. He had the lead in a character study about a much-decorated war hero with marital problems. Tracy was enthusiastic about the script and plunged into it. The part

21

of Richard Banks provided an opportunity to depict such contrasting qualities as "humility, patience, bravado, swagger, pugnacity, generosity, and resignation." He took over the role during the Boston tryout after it had been vacated by Clark Gable.

Conflict opened on March 6 at the Fulton Theater and lasted only thirty-seven performances. Although Tracy's personal notices were excellent, reviews were dismal. *Conflict* was a bitter disappointment. Tracy felt that his career on Broadway had come to a standstill.

His next play, *Nigger Rich* (subtitled *The Big Shot*), was another drama about returning war veterans. He didn't have the lead, but merely supported Eric Dressler, who played a heel sponging on his buddies. *Nigger Rich* was a quick failure (eleven performances) at the Royale after its September 26 opening.

Dread at least restored Tracy to a leading role. Once again he was a World War I hero, this time a scoundrel who betrays countless women but goes insane when the spirit of one of his victims returns to haunt him. This wildly improbable melodrama had a good cast that included Madge Evans, George Meeker, and Helen Mack. *Dread* tried out in Washington and then played Brooklyn's Majestic Theater for a week. The producers decided not to risk Broadway.

Compared to *Dread*, Hugh Stange's *Veneer* was a well-written, if downbeat, slice of New York life that opened at the Sam H. Harris Theater on November 12, 1929, with Joanna Roos and Henry Hull in the leading roles. During its one-month run, Tracy replaced Hull on Broadway. The part of Charlie Riggs was completely unsympathetic, but it was sharply defined and Tracy was able to vitalize a believable character effectively. He played a cheap braggart who seduces, then walks out on, a näive girl. Three years later, Helen Twelvetrees and Eric Linden costarred in a bowdlerized movie version of *Veneer* entitled *The Young Bride*.

All this theatrical activity in one year added up to nothing. The stock-market crash seemed to be an ominous threat to the once-thriving New York theater, and actors who had not succeeded were in a precarious position.

By the end of 1929, Tracy's morale was at its lowest ebb. He missed out on several roles he wanted because producers didn't consider him a matinee-idol type. Still under thirty, he looked

With James Bell in stage production of THE LAST MILE (1930)

too young for mature character parts.

This was the era in which Hollywood raided Broadway in a search for new "talkie" stars. Many stage performers were signed to lucrative contracts. Tracy was among those who were tested in New York for films, but no movie offers resulted. The general opinion was that he didn't photograph well and was not a good bet for screen stardom.

Once more, Tracy was ready to give up the struggle. But his long-elusive breakthrough in the theater was just ahead. He won the pivotal role of Killer John Mears in John Wexley's grimly realistic prison melodrama *The Last Mile*. Tracy was not at all confident of the play's ultimate success or his own performance in it when *The Last Mile* went into rehearsal. There was very little advance interest, and it would be competing with another prison play, *The Criminal Code*, which was one of the most acclaimed productions of the 1929-30 season.

But the concern proved to be unwarranted. In 1930, the play's stark, brutal realism and blunt dialogue, electrified the New York theater critics who used every superlative in their glowing reviews when the play opened at the Sam H. Harris Theater on February 13. There was no doubt about the show's artistic merit, but some reservations as to whether it would win popular approval. The critics were wrong in this respect. *The Last Mile* was an immediate hit and the dramatic sensation of the season.

All the principal players, as well as young newcomer Chester Erskine's assured direction, were praised. None more so than Tracy, whose dynamic portrayal of a cold-blooded convict riveted audience attention from beginning to end. This personal triumph lifted Tracy to prominence as a serious actor. His previous reputation in the theater had rested chiefly on his skillful delineation of a light-comedy role in *The Baby Cyclone*.

The Last Mile describes Mears as "hard as nails, medium height; wiry; narrow, hard eyes; narrow mouth; illiterate, but intelligent; dominant." Tracy projected all these characteristics in an uncompromising, chilling performance. He was the personification of the antihero, but with recognizable traces of humanity and compassion.

While he was playing in *The Last Mile*, Tracy picked up some extra money by appearing in at least two short films produced at Warner Brothers' Vitaphone studios in Brooklyn. They were directed by Arthur Hurley, who was entrusted with most of the dramatic one- and two-reelers turned out in that studio. Hurley drew upon Broadway theatrical talent almost exclusively for his casts.

Tracy's first short, *Taxi Talks*, marked his movie debut. Released in June 1930 it offered a series of vignettes involving a cabdriver (Vernon Wallace) being questioned by the police. He describes the occurrences in his cab, climaxed by a murder. Tracy appeared as a mobster who is knifed to death by his hysterically jealous girlfriend (Katherine Alexander). The cast included other players on their way up: Evalyn Knapp, Roger Pryor, and Mayo Methot. Tracy also starred in Vitaphone's ten-minute "miniature drama," *The Hard Guy* (also 1930). Here, in a simple story with an O'Henry twist, he played a war veteran down on his luck who appears to be planning a robbery with his old Army pistol. It turns out he was merely pawning the gun. (Katherine Alexander was his worried wife.)°

John Ford, already a veteran director in 1930, saw a performance of *The Last Mile* during a visit to New York. He was so impressed with the production and with Tracy's fine acting that he returned several times. Ford persuaded Fox Studios to sign Tracy for a leading role in *Up the River*, a prison story he was planning to direct. Tracy was finally acting in a feature film.

°Tracy may also have appeared in a Vitaphone one-reel prison tale called *The Strong Arm*. But his name is not listed in that film's official credits.

Fox offered Tracy a one-picture deal—one thousand dollars a week for six weeks' work. He obtained a leave of absence from *The Last Mile*, and Thomas Mitchell replaced him as Mears. In June 1930 Spencer Tracy was on his way to Hollywood.

Up the River was originally intended to be a serious study of prison life. But Maurine Watkins's screenplay was ultimately rejected. The reason: MGM's prison drama, *The Big House*, was a sensational success and Ford did not want to make a carbon copy.

For a time, Fox thought of abandoning *Up the River*. Then Ford decided to keep the bare bones of the script and turn it into a comedy. William Collier, Sr., a member of the cast, assisted Ford in writing gags and new dialogue, which delayed the start of production. Ford had to rush Tracy through his scenes so he could return to New York and *The Last Mile* on time.

An hilarious, irreverent spoof of prison pictures and the penal system in general, *Up the River* centers on two hardboiled but likable crooks—St. Louis (Tracy) and Dannemora Dan (Warren Hymer)—who are expert jailbreakers. St. Louis is a swaggering "big shot"; Dan is a good-natured dope. To their cha-

THE YEARS AT FOX (1930-1935)

grin, they find themselves in Bensonata, a coed prison with a collegiate atmosphere where, in a marvelously comic sequence, St. Louis is welcomed back to the criminal community. He arrives in sartorial splendor, wearing an immaculately tailored striped suit with derby and cane. There is a reception by the carefree convicts, newsreel men, reporters who want to interview him, a brass band, and a friendly warden who all but gives him the keys to the jail. St. Louis expresses his appreciation, and then announces that he has every intention of leaving "as soon as I look over the layout."

The film derives much of its humor from the inmates' obsession with baseball, and the determination of the team manager, Pop (William Collier, Sr.), to win the interpenitentiary cup. St. Louis turns out to be as good a pitcher as he is a jailbreaker. The only complication: St. Louis and Dan are required to break out of jail long enough to help an ex-convict friend (Humphrey Bogart, in his second film), who is in serious trouble. "There's too

UP THE RIVER (1930). With Warren Hymer and Humphrey Bogart

much fresh air" on the outside, St. Louis and Dan tell each other as they return to prison in time to win the big game for Bensonata.

Up the River was an unexpected hit. Some critics called it one of the best comedies of the year. The picture was an auspicious start for Tracy. It is easy to see Tracy's special quality surfac-ing in this early effort. His characterization develops as the movie progresses, from conscienceless braggart to warmly appealing hero.

On the strength of his first movie, Fox was sure that Tracy was going to be a major star. The studio had ambitious plans for him, and signed him to a five-year contract. When *The Last*

QUICK MILLIONS (1931). As "Bugs" Raymond

Mile closed, Tracy moved his family to Hollywood permanently.

Tracy's next film was a change of pace from the broad slapstick of *Up the River*. Fox cast him in *Quick Millions* (1931), its contribution to the popular gangster cycle that began with *Little Caesar* early that year. It was directed and coauthored by Rowland Brown, who was responsible for the script of *Doorway to Hell*, an earlier underworld drama in which James Cagney made his second film appearance. It was Brown's first effort at directing, and a few discerning critics predicted a notable future for him. A majority of the critics, however, were disappointed in the film, finding some of the action difficult to follow and some of the characters inexplicable. Today, *Quick Millions* is considered a classic in its genre, and Brown has received his due as a director with fresh and original ideas. But in 1931, his style was too remote for the general public, and the film did not attract a wide audience. All the reviewers did praise Tracy for his vivid, arresting portrayal of Bugs Raymond.

Tracy's interpretation of a gangster is substantially different from the nasty, snarling hoodlums played by James Cagney and Edward G. Robinson the same year. His antihero is intelligent, quick-witted, and far from illiterate. Although hot-tempered and handy with his fists, he prefers to use his brain rather than his brawn. He is forceful and magnetic, the epitome of the self-made man, and he would not be out of place in the high society he aspires to. Another wrongly "Forgotten Film", *Quick Millions* also contains one of Tracy's outstanding performances of the thirties.

The film depicts the rise and fall of Daniel J. ("Bugs") Raymond, an ambitious truckdriver who rises to become a rich and powerful figure in the rackets, acquiring along the way an equally powerful and even more vicious enemy in "Nails" Markey (Warner Richmond). In the expected fashion, he also tangles with two women: Daisy (Sally Eilers), the "moll" he casually deserts for Dorothy (Marguerite Churchill), an initially cool but later intrigued debutante he plans to marry for "prestige." Two scenes stand out in the film: one in which Bugs delivers a sudden blow to Daisy's chin (a scene as startling as Cagney's famous grapefruit thrust on Mae Clarke in *The Public Enemy*); and the grimly ironic final scene in which Bugs, attempting to prevent

Early portrait

Dorothy's marriage to another man, is killed by Nails on the way to the church. One of Nails's men remarks on how fancy society weddings are. "Yeah," his companion replies, "but us hoodlums have the swell funerals." It is the last line in the film.

When *Quick Millions* failed at the box office, Fox apparently lost interest in promoting Tracy as a new star. Choice roles went to other actors. Instead, Tracy was assigned to a series of routine B movies. Stories about his frustration over the pictures he was getting, clashes with top Fox executives, the wild drinking binges, and frequent disappearances from the studio for days at a time are now part of the Tracy legend. But his personal anguish does not show on the screen. He took enough pride in his work to give the best in him to the worst of his films.

Today, all of Tracy's Fox pictures have nostalgic interest. Many are entertaining, and some are unusually good. And every one of them is the better for the excellent Tracy performances they contain.

A good example is *Six Cylinder Love* (1931), which followed *Quick Millions*. This was an inconsequential comedy adapted from an old stage play. Although he received top billing, Tracy's

SIX CYLINDER LOVE (1931). With Sidney Fox and Lorin Raker

role was a supporting one. He played William Donroy, a slick, high-pressure salesman who sells an expensive car to a middle-aged couple. The auto attracts so many sponging friends that the husband goes bankrupt. He persuades Donroy to sell the car to a younger couple. The pattern is repeated. Finally, with Donroy's help, the new owner is able to find a third buyer for the troublesome car. This time it's an eccentric janitor with loads of cash.

Despite his limited footage, Tracy made every scene count. He was at his jaunty best when called upon to do a bit of flirting with the film's leading ladies, Sidney Fox and Una Merkel.

Since Tracy and Warren Hymer had worked so well together in *Up the River*, Fox thought they might make a good comedy team. The vehicle selected for them was *Goldie* (1931), a sound remake of the 1928 Howard Hawks silent movie, *A Girl in Every Port*. Jean Harlow, then under contract to producer Howard Hughes, was borrowed for the title role.

Relying heavily on broad, racy humor, *Goldie* cast Tracy and Hymer as two sailors famous for their amorous adventures in waterfront towns from Russia to South America. In Calais, they become involved with Goldie, a carnival high diver. Spike

GOLDIE (1931). With Warren Hymer and Jean Harlow

(Hymer) falls for her, though Bill (Tracy) warns him that she is a gold-digger he knew back in Brooklyn. Goldie succeeds in breaking up their friendship, though the pals are reunited in the end. As the film closes, they are exchanging promises. Spike: "And we swear off dames for good!" Bill: "Yeah, and we start right now!" Spike: "No, let's wait till tomorrow."

Goldie was fairly popular, but further plans to feature Tracy and Hymer in other films were abandoned. Harlow, not yet the sparkling comedienne of later years, still had a lot to learn about acting.

In July 1931 Tracy started

work on *She Wanted a Millionaire* (1932), opposite Joan Bennett, a promising young actress on the Fox lot. Halfway through production, Bennett was thrown from a horse during location filming. The picture shut down for five months while she recuperated from her injuries. By the time they resumed in December, Tracy had completed another movie while on loan to Howard Hughes.

She Wanted a Millionaire was the first of the so-called women's pictures in Tracy's career. His function was to provide the chief support and romantic interest to Bennett, who played a beauty-contest winner who mar-

ries a wealthy roué. The film begins as light comedy and then veers into lurid melodrama as Bennett learns that her husband is a sadistic, insanely jealous psychopath who ruthlessly subjects her to countless indignities. Tracy played Bennett's hometown admirer, a breezy young engineer who rekindles a romance with the abused wife. The climax comes when Bennett's husband, surprisingly gracious about granting her a divorce so that she can marry Tracy, tries to throw her into a cage filled with hungry Great Danes. He is shot down by one of his servants, and Tracy and Bennett are reunited for a happy ending.

SKY DEVILS (1932). With Billy Bevan

Most critics found it impossible to take this absurd plot seriously. But as one reviewer wrote: "Tracy gives the picture its most interesting moments, wisecracking in peppy fashion, turning romantic when necessary and always giving evidence of the swell actor he is."

Sky Devils (1932), the film Tracy made for Howard Hughes, was a takeoff on both *What Price Glory?* and Hughes's famous air epic *Hell's Angels*. Seven writers, including its director Edward Sutherland, worked on the script, but the attempt to combine slapstick farce with thrilling serial stunts didn't work. *Sky Devils*, despite some funny scenes and spectacular aviation photography, missed the mark as acceptable screen entertainment.

Tracy was once again a cocky wise guy, this time becoming reluctantly involved with World War I. Overseas, he battles with a tough sergeant (William Boyd) for the love of an American girl (Ann Dvorak) but the three-cornered romance takes a back seat to mock melodrama as the trio is caught up in a series of comic misadventures that ends with their being arrested as spies. Following much hectic activity, including Tracy's unintentional destruction of a German munitions dump, the two men and a girl are rescued by an entire US squadron. Flying home to a celebration in their honor, Tracy accidentally steps on the bomb release. Officers and men scatter, and the headquarters is demolished. "What will we do now?" Boyd asks. "Keep right on going," Tracy answers as they continue their flight.

Tracy completed his first full year in pictures with *Sky Devils* and *She Wanted a Millionaire*. He continued to be a workhorse in 1932, making six films for his home studio and *20,000 Years in Sing Sing* for First National.

His next film, *Disorderly Conduct*, was an implausible melodrama, but it offered Tracy a strong role as an honest motorcycle cop who allows himself to be corrupted by gangsters, bootleggers, and gamblers. He tangles with his captain (Ralph Bellamy) and with the insolent daughter (Sally Eilers) of a crooked politician, who is being courted by the captain. Predictably, after much skulduggery involving bribery and murder, Tracy reforms when the bullet meant to assassinate him strikes his little nephew instead. At the end, Tracy is back on his motorcycle, he and Bellamy are friends, and Sally indicates clearly that she is growing fond of

DISORDERLY CONDUCT (1932). With Sally Eilers

Con-1-24

YOUNG AMERICA (1932).
As Jack Doray

Spencer Tracy.

Tracy and Ralph Bellamy were then reunited in *Young America*. This was a sentimental drama of small-town life, directed by Frank Borzage with his customary skill and care. Tracy played the town druggist, and Bellamy a judge. *Young America* was intended to sound a warning: wayward boys needed understanding, and they could be turned into criminals by being sent to reformatories. The film placed the responsibility for guidance on individual communities. (In some ways, *Young America* might be called a forerunner to *Boys Town*.) The acting was good, but as a social document the film's effectiveness was weakened by a screenplay that often strained credulity.

The movie centered on the misfortunes of a well-meaning youngster (Tommy Conlon), who has a reputation for being "the worst kid in town." He breaks into Tracy's drugstore to steal medicine for a friend's sick grandmother. Indignant and unrelenting, Tracy demands that the boy be punished, but by the end of the film young Conlon wins Tracy's respect when he risks his life to apprehend crooks who have robbed the store. The film was routine drama, but Borzage's characteristic ability to extract convincing performances from his cast was evident throughout.

With its emphasis on a strong male friendship being disrupted by a woman, Tracy's next film — *Society Girl* — predates the kind of movies Tracy later made at MGM with Clark Gable. Tracy played the combination big brother, protector, and nursemaid to an up-and-coming prizefighter (James Dunn, Fox's new big bet for stardom). Dunn falls in love with a debutante (Peggy Shannon) who has only a casual interest in him.

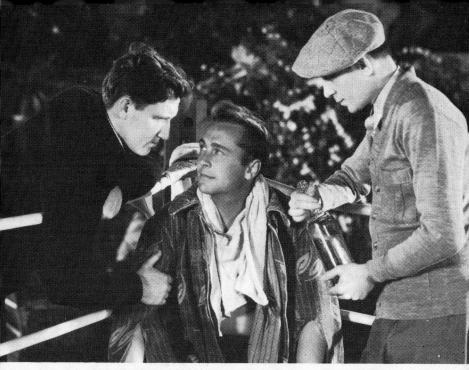

SOCIETY GIRL (1932). With James Dunn and Bert Hanlon

The friends quarrel and separate when Dunn refuses to give up the girl. Dunn's boxing condition deteriorates when he learns that Tracy was right all along, but the devoted manager succeeds in getting the repentant boxer back into shape. All this familiar hokum was directed disinterestedly by Sidney Lanfield.

In *The Painted Woman*, Tracy and William Boyd were again battling over a woman— this time in a melodrama almost as ludicrous as *She Wanted a Millionaire*. Disregarding the earlier films, the new movie was advertised as featuring Tracy in "his first romantic role." The studio's "two-fisted, he-man" actor played an ex-Marine engaged in the pearl-diving business in the South Seas. He meets and marries a café entertainer (Peggy Shannon, as a watered-down Sadie Thompson), who has previously been involved with the captain of a schooner (Boyd). When the captain returns to claim her, the two men clash. Later, when the girl is arrested for murdering Boyd, Tracy re-

37

ME AND MY GIRL (1932). With Joan Bennett

fuses to help her, believing "the worst." But the two are reconciled when Tracy learns that Boyd was killed by a native diver.

This compilation of clichés had a few interesting moments. There is one exciting scene of Tracy rescuing his diver from a particularly ferocious octopus. And Tracy and Boyd made their big confrontation crackle with tension. As usual, Tracy received the best reviews. A typical example: "Tracy as the jolly, gallant ex-Marine is so vigorous, expert,

and agreeable, he almost makes you believe in the melodrama he is forced to present."

Me and My Gal, Tracy's last film released in 1932, might have been an ordinary cops-and-robbers melodrama. What makes it different is the snappy, wisecracking romance of a happy-go-lucky police detective and a slangy cashier in a waterfront restaurant, which counterpoints the action throughout the film. Raoul Walsh's breezy direction and the zestful performances of Tracy and Joan Bennett (in a decided change of pace) contribute to the overall effect. This modest film retains much of its original sparkle and is still highly enjoyable.

The film is studded with the sort of brash, flavorsome quips typical of movies in the thirties. Dan (Tracy) meets Helen (Bennett) while on duty. He is immediately smitten and starts a flirtation. "Didn't I meet you somewhere?" he asks. "I've been somewhere," she answers. But Dan is not intimidated and wastes no time in wooing Helen. He tells her he's tired of drinking twenty cups of coffee a day and asks for a date. "How would you like to go over to the park and help me tramp down the flowers?" Helen: "With feet like yours, you don't need help." Dan reflects upon his predicament as Helen resists his advances. "Some girls are like motors. You've got to choke them to get them started. She's fresh, she's saucy, she bosses me around, but I'm crazy about her."

Halfway through the picture, Helen decides that she really loves Dan. She invites him over for an evening. This scene is a highlight, since it includes a funny and unexpected spoof of Eugene O'Neill's *Strange Interlude*, which had recently been filmed with many of the stage version's interior monologues intact. They have both seen a movie called *Strange Innertube*, and are discussing it. The conversation is interspersed with their private thoughts, spoken on the soundtrack. Dan: "A guy don't know what to do . . . if I don't neck, I'm too slow. And if I do neck, you think I'm fresh." Helen: "A girl don't know what to do. If she lets a guy maul her, he thinks she's no good. And if she doesn't, he thinks she's old-fashioned."

While all this is going on, a melodramatic stew is boiling involving Helen's married sister, Kate (Marion Burns). Before her marriage, Kate had an affair with Duke, a gangster (played by George Walsh, director Raoul Walsh's brother). He breaks out of jail and forces Kate to hide him in her attic. There he plans a successful bank robbery with his gang. Kate's husband is away on a freighter but her father-in-law Sarge (Henry B. Walthall), a paralyzed war veteran who cannot speak and can only move his eyes, is witness to the situation. When Dan and Helen come to tell Kate that they are engaged, Sarge is able to telegraph a Morse code message to Dan with his blinking eyes. Dan captures Duke, recovers the stolen money,

20,000 YEARS IN SING SING (1933). With Arthur Byron

collects a reward, and takes Helen on a honeymoon trip to Bermuda.

A suspense thriller so generously sprinkled with amusing dialogue was a novelty in 1932, and *Me and My Gal* did surprisingly well at the box office. Tracy gave further evidence of his developing talents by turning a standard roughneck role into a unique characterization.

20,000 Years in Sing Sing (1933), which he made on loan to Warners-First National, was also successful. Director Michael Curtiz requested Tracy for the lead, and the fact that it was some-

thing of a prestige production was highly gratifying to the aspiring young film actor. The film was suggested by a best-selling book by Lewis E. Lawes, warden of the Ossining, New York, prison (Sing Sing). Incidents that actually occurred at Sing Sing, such as an attempted jailbreak, were incorporated into an otherwise fictional script, which took many liberties with the established rules and regulations of the institution. The final film, despite its authentic atmosphere, emerged as a fast-moving but overly contrived crime melodrama typical of the period.

The impressive opening montage of prisoners and numbers sets the proper mood. This footage, and the accompanying ground and aerial shots, was filmed on location at Ossining. Sets built in Hollywood were duplicated from still photographs.

In the early scenes, Tracy's tough, brash, independent-minded gangster is not unlike the character he played in *Up the River*. On the train taking him to Sing Sing, where he is to serve five to thirty years, he is full of bravado. "Nobody can take my place," he says. "I got color, I got personality." At the prison gates, he is given a celebrity's reception by reporters, photographers, and admirers.

On the inside, it's a different story. Tracy is defiant with the prison guards; refusing to wear an oversized uniform and appearing in the yard in his underwear, he is thrown into the icehouse. He is belligerent with the stern but humane warden (Arthur Byron). "If I had a chance to break out of here and rub someone out to do it," Tracy tells him, "I'd just as soon rub you out." The warden places him in solitary confinement, and later puts him to work on a rock pile.

Tracy refuses to join a prison break (a brilliantly executed sequence) because it falls on a Saturday. "All the bad breaks that ever happened to me happened on a Saturday." On this jinx day, he was "born, arrested, brought to trial, convicted, and delivered to Sing Sing." His only warm feelings are reserved for his mistress, played by the young Bette Davis.

Tracy's arrogance gradually changes under the benevolent influence of the warden and he becomes a model prisoner. But then his luck turns sour again: the warden tells him that Davis has been seriously injured in an accident and may be dying. Tracy begs to be allowed to visit her and is released temporarily on the honor system, promising to return immediately afterward. He is, however, apprehensive because it is Saturday.

In Davis's apartment, Tracy learns that she had jumped from a car while trying to resist the advances of his crooked lawyer (Louis Calhern). During Tracy's scuffle with the lawyer, Davis shoots him from her bed. Tracy takes the blame for the killing and flees with the help of underworld friends. But when he reads in the papers that the warden has been severely criticized for releasing him and is being forced

FACE IN THE SKY (1933). With Marian Nixon and Stuart Erwin

to resign, he returns to Sing Sing. "I told you I'd come back even if it meant the chair," is his greeting to the warden.

Tracy is convicted of murder and sentenced to die. No one will believe his girl's story, which he firmly denies. When Davis comes to his cell, just before his execution, he tries to comfort her. "This is a chance to do something decent in my life. You can't take that away from me." The film ends as it began, with a montage of men and numbers.

According to the critics, Tracy's portrayal was the movie's principal distinction. He was now considered one of the best actors on the screen. Scenes of Tracy, brooding alone in his cell, had an intensity that lingered in the viewer's memory. Warren Hymer, now reduced to small roles, was also in *20,000 Years in Sing Sing*. He did his familiar feeble-minded act, playing the harmonica as he is led to the electric chair.

Tracy returned to Fox and *Face in the Sky* (1933), an excursion into whimsical romance. This modern Cinderella story was not particularly well received at the time, but it had a certain charm. Tracy played an idealistic sign painter who considers himself as great an artist as Michelangelo, though he confines his work to signs advertising beauty cream. Marian Nixon was the mistreated farm girl who loves and then loses him, only to find him again in a most improbable ending. Tracy is commissioned to paint a huge sign atop a skyscraper representing "the most beautiful woman in the world." His inspiration is supposed to be a haughty society girl (Lila Lee), but he is haunted by visions of the farm girl. The grand unveiling of his sign is given all the glamour of a movie premiere. When the girl views the proceedings through a telescope, she sees her "face in the sky" and knows she has found Tracy. She rushes to him for a predictable happy ending.

Far more important to Tracy than any of his 1932 films

was the birth of his daughter, Louise—nicknamed Susie—on July 1 of that year. Tracy was fearful throughout his wife's pregnancy that their second child might also be born deaf. When she turned out to be a healthy, normal child, Tracy was elated. The Tracys were then living on a seven-and-a-half-acre ranch in Encino, California. Tracy's mother and brother, Carroll, came west to be with them. Carroll would remain Spencer's business manager until the actor's death in 1967.

The tragedy of his son's deafness still continued to plague him, affecting his career and his marriage. Work in motion pictures brought financial security, but although he could afford the best doctors, they could not find a cure. Since giving up the stage, Mrs. Tracy had set out to learn everything she could about congenital deafness. She consulted countless doctors and, in time, became an expert on the subject herself. Tracy's problems were secondary. His wife had little time to devote to him and he did not expect more of her. He tried to help Mrs. Tracy teach the boy to talk and "hear," but he lacked the necessary patience. And he could not shake guilt feelings that he was somehow to blame for John's affliction. The result-

ing strains and tensions took their toll. They led him to spend his leisure time drinking—away from home. His drinking eventually got out of hand.

Resentment over some of his film assignments also contributed to his depression. He fought violently with directors and producers about scripts he considered badly written or dishonest. Often he would disappear during production of a picture, and the studio was obliged to call in the police to search for him across the country. He once wrecked a sound stage on which Fox production chief Winfield Sheehan had locked him overnight—to sleep off his intoxication.

Tracy did manage to pull himself together for long periods. He developed saner leisure-time interests. He had a natural love of horses, and, at Will Rogers's suggestion, took up polo.

Nineteen thirty-three was a better year for Tracy. There were several films that he flatly refused to do, but two assignments were rewarding and one of them proved to be a milestone in his career.

Producer Jesse L. Lasky, formerly a top Paramount executive, had recently joined Fox with his own production unit. Lasky admired Tracy as an actor. He first cast him in a picture called *Helldorado*, but Tracy disappeared before the start of production and had to be replaced with Richard Arlen. Lasky gave Tracy another chance.

The producer was extremely enthusiastic about *The Power and the Glory*, a screenplay by Preston Sturges, a young playwright who had had some success on the stage and had joined the Paramount writing staff. The story was not unusual, but Sturges's treatment was startling in its originality. The events of a man's life were told via flashbacks that were out of chronological order, a technique later used by Orson Welles in *Citizen Kane*.

The Power and the Glory was going to be a major production. Fox held out for a bigger box-office name, but Lasky insisted on having Tracy for the lead. Tracy himself had misgivings about the role, which required him to go from youth to old age. It was his most demanding part to date, and the success or failure of the film could depend on his performance. He put all his resources into the character he was creating, and both Lasky and director William K. Howard were tremendously moved by his work during the filming.

Sturges, incidentally, cut his directorial teeth on this picture, serving as assistant dialogue director. His detailed screenplay contained specific instructions for cameraman and editor—an innovation at the time. Lasky shot the movie exactly as Sturges wrote it.

The Power and the Glory is a somber, ironic psychological study of a man who achieved great wealth and suffered shattering disillusionment in his personal life. The film opens with the funeral of Tom Garner (Tracy), the thoroughly disliked president of the Chicago and Southwestern Railway. Only Henry (Ralph Morgan), his private secretary and lifelong friend, remembers him with affection, and it is he who narrates the picture throughout, his voice connecting the various episodes, as he tries to explain Tom to his disapproving wife. She considers the dead man to have been a ruthless egotist. Incidents are depicted, not in continuity, but as they naturally occur to Henry in answer to his wife's accusations. Henry skips back and forth through the years, and almost every scene contains his running commentary. "The power and the glory, what they can do to a man. It just happened to him, like everything else happened to him."

THE POWER AND THE GLORY (1933). With Colleen Moore

Henry recalls the time they were boys together, and how Tom, a born leader, saved him from drowning in "the old swimming hole." Later, we see Tom as a young railroad track walker, who confesses to Sally (Colleen Moore), a schoolteacher, that he cannot read or write. She tutors him and Tom's hesitant courtship leads to a marriage proposal. This charming scene, played on a country hill, is narrated completely by Henry, but the words he speaks synchronize with Tom and Sally's lip movements.

Sally is a loyal but ambitious wife. She wants Tom to advance in the world, and track-walks for him while he goes to night school and learns about railroads. They have a son. Tom wins a promotion and gradually moves through various jobs in the railway company until he becomes president.

In his middle years, as his company expands, Tom falls in love with Eve, (Helen Vinson), a business associate's daughter. When he asks Sally for a divorce, she commits suicide in quiet despair. Before she dies, she tells Tom: "And why shouldn't you be in love, and why shouldn't you do what you want to do for once before you die."

Sally's death precipitates the mounting tragedy. Tom's son and second wife have an affair and she gives birth to a child. Tom believes that he is the father, but when he discovers the truth he also commits suicide.

The Power and the Glory is another early Tracy picture that is now regarded as a classic. It was his first "special," and Fox held up its release for five months in order to launch the film with appropriate fanfare. In the promotional buildup, the storytelling device combining flashbacks and offscreen commentary was called narratage. The studio was sure they had a winner and gave Tracy a new contract that would run to 1937.

Narratage failed to revolutionize screen technique in the early thirties, and the movie, because of its downbeat theme, did not live up to expectations at the box office. Reviews, however, were generally favorable, and unanimous in their praise of Tracy and Colleen Moore. Tom Garner was not a very sympathetic character, but Tracy's much-admired performance made him a believable person—engaging, dominant, and ultimately pitiful.

Frank Borzage, a close personal friend of Tracy's, was now working at Columbia. During his seven years at Fox, Borzage had become one of Hollywood's most valued directors, winning two Academy Awards—for *Seventh Heaven* and *Bad Girl*. He had wanted Tracy for the latter film, but the actor lost out to James Dunn. Borzage now requested Tracy for the male lead in *Man's Castle*. Fox was willing and Tracy was delighted.

Borzage's forte was sentimental romantic drama. *Man's Castle* had some of the bittersweet poignancy of *Seventh Heaven*, but it was also one of the first films to attempt a realistic depiction of America's Depression era. Its setting of a waterfront shantytown, with its tumbledown shacks and pitiful derelicts, was suitably grim, and

MAN'S CASTLE (1933). With Loretta Young

to soften the harsher aspects of his story, Borzage made his principal characters—the gruff, irresponsible Bill and the wistful, lovely Trina—as appealing as Chico and Diane in *Seventh Heaven.* Tracy's costar was the beautiful Loretta Young, just twenty-one and already a veteran leading lady. Their performances helped make *Man's Castle* a memorable and successful movie. It was also a surprisingly adult picture for its time. Borzage was forced to make certain revisions demanded by the censors.

Bill and Trina are two poverty-stricken young people who meet in the park one evening. Bill is deceptively dressed in top-hat, white tie, and tails, but his illuminated shirt tells us that he is only a walking advertisement for a brand of coffee. Trina is homeless and half-starved. Bill takes pity on Trina and brings her to his shack. "When people got nothin', they act like human beings," he tells her in a typical remark.

Trina is happy and tries to make a home for Bill, but he wants it understood that it is only a temporary arrangement. He is a wanderer and intends to take off just as soon as he has a little money. Trina assures Bill that she has no claim on him.

Bill's tough exterior hides the proverbial heart of gold, and when he finds out that Trina is pregnant, he agrees to marry her just to give the child a name. Then he will leave. To get some money for Trina, he tries to rob a toy factory where his friend Ira (Walter Connolly) is the night watchman. Bill is wounded by Ira, who allows him to escape. But by this time Bill realizes how much Trina means to him. The two hop a freight train to face an uncertain future together.

Tracy and Loretta Young fell in love while filming *Man's Castle*. He moved out of his ranch home to live at the Riviera Club, where the polo matches were held. Shortly thereafter, Mrs. Tracy announced that she and her husband had decided on a trial separation because of incompatibility.

The Tracy-Young romance received a good deal of publicity. Finally, after more than a year, Miss Young brought the situation to a conclusion. She issued the following statement to the press: "Since Spencer Tracy and I are both Catholic and can never be married, we have agreed not to

SHANGHAI MADNESS (1933). With Fay Wray and Maude Eburne

see each other again." The Tracys were reconciled and he moved back to the ranch.

Man's Castle premiered in November 1933. By that time, Tracy had completed two films at Fox that were released before the Columbia picture. He wasn't happy with either of them, but they were bigger moneymakers than *The Power and the Glory*.

The first, *Shanghai Madness*, was a standard adventure yarn with an Oriental background very much in vogue at the time. Every studio was trying to duplicate the success of Paramount's *Shanghai Express* in which an exotic Marlene Dietrich had confronted a cruel Chinese warlord. Fay Wray, fresh from the arms of King Kong, supplied the heavy love interest.

Shanghai Madness advances the preposterous idea that Tracy, as a Naval officer in China during the Chinese Civil War, could be dishonorably discharged from the service for attacking a Communist stronghold after they had fired at his ship and killed some of his men. He spends a great deal of time brooding about this shabby treatment until he meets a beautiful girl named Wildeth Christie (Wray), who begins to pursue him relentlessly. When he decides to do a bit of gunrunning on the Chinese coast, she

stows away on his riverboat to be with him. After a number of improbable incidents, the climax comes when Tracy and his crew engage in heroic hand-to-hand combat to rescue Wildeth from a US mission being fired upon by a band of Communists. Tracy, of course, is now restored to his position of honor in the Navy. The actor performed his absurd role with proper dash and virility, and seemed to enjoy playing opposite Fay Wray.

The Mad Game was a much more interesting film. It had several clever plot twists and gave Tracy a meaty role that he could really enjoy playing. Long before his appearance in *Dr. Jekyll and Mr. Hyde*, this picture required Tracy to use makeup that completely disguised his regular features. It was another gangster melodrama with an incredible plot, but the acting and direction were first-rate, and *The Mad Game* emerged as a suspenseful, fast-moving entertainment. The film was also the first to deal with kidnapping and was undoubtedly inspired by the public furor over the tragic Lindbergh case.

Tracy played an imprisoned bootlegger who learns that his old gang has, with the end of Prohibition, switched from illegal liquor to kidnapping. Enraged

THE MAD GAME (1933). With Kathleen Burke

LOOKING FOR TROUBLE (1934). With Jack Oakie (hands raised)

because, years ago, his own daughter had been a victim of "the snatch game," Tracy decides to help the government. When the son and daughter-in-law of a prominent judge are kidnapped, Tracy convinces the warden to parole him long enough to bring the criminals to justice. He submits to plastic surgery. With altered features and a new name and identity, Tracy is unrecognized by his former associates. He is able to rescue the kidnap victims, but he is shot in the ensuing gunbattle and dies in the arms of his former sweetheart (Claire Trevor).

The film would have been ridiculous if Tracy had not been absolutely convincing in the second phase of the character-ization. The makeup job, though hardly flattering, was uncanny, and Tracy submerged his familiar personality and vocal projection with brilliant results. His acting is so effective that if a viewer saw only the last half of the film, he would not realize that Spencer Tracy was playing the role.

More than ever, critics insisted that Tracy should be getting better scripts. But Fox, fully aware of his talent, believed that the failure of *The Power and the Glory* was mainly due to his lack of box-office appeal. And, because of his increasingly erratic personal conduct, they were reluctant to give him a major assignment until he regained control of himself.

Tracy was now farmed out to Darryl F. Zanuck's new production company, 20th Century, then releasing through United Artists. The picture—*Looking for Trouble*—was an unimportant comedy-melodrama, but it had the advantages of a good cast and William A. Wellman's brisk direction. Tracy and Jack Oakie appeared as two happy-go-lucky Los Angeles telephone repairmen, with Constance Cummings and Arline Judge as their respective girlfriends.

Tracy and Cummings quarrel continuously because she refuses to believe that her boss is both a wiretapper and a bank robber. This versatile villain is subsequently killed by his old flame, a sexy blonde who also has a yen for Tracy. She is provocatively played by Judith Wood in the Jean Harlow manner. Cummings is arrested for the murder. A climactic earthquake sequence enables Tracy to get a confession from Wood before she dies. Exceptionally well-done special effects make these earthquake scenes the highlight of the movie.

Tracy had reason to be

THE SHOW-OFF (1934). With Madge Evans

grateful for the next occasion he was loaned out, which proved to be a turning point in his career. MGM borrowed him for the lead in *The Show-Off*, an adaptation of George Kelly's famous play. The studio originally bought the screen rights from Paramount for Lee Tracy, who had appeared in a supporting role in the original 1924 stage production. But Tracy got into trouble with the Mexican government for supposedly insulting its army during location filming on *Viva Villa!* Louis B. Mayer fired him and tested scores of actors for the part of Aubrey Piper. No one seemed right. In January 1934 MGM was almost ready to abandon the project. They finally decided on Spencer Tracy for the coveted role. *The Show-Off* was Tracy's introduction to MGM. Producer Irving Thalberg was so impressed with his work that he told the actor he hoped to acquire his services in the future. And Tracy found the atmosphere at MGM more congenial than at Fox.

Tracy's performance was enthusiastically reviewed, and for the first time his name appeared alone above the title of the picture. *The Show-Off* opened at New York's Capitol Theater in March 1934 and was held over a second week, which was then un-usual for a modest production. The movie did excellent business throughout the country.

In this endearingly funny little film, Tracy is the quintessence of all loud-mouthed, boasting, obnoxious braggarts. The new script also made him lovable and sympathetic, which is not the way playwright Kelly had conceived the character. But it may explain why this film enjoyed greater popularity than two previous screen versions.

J. Aubrey Piper is only a thirty-two-dollar-a-week clerk in a railroad company, but he acts as if he were the vice president. At the office, this master of bombast is full of wild schemes. When nobody pays any attention to him, he feels his business talents are unappreciated. Scornful of his superiors, he thinks the company manager is "a dodo who should have retired long ago." His favorite catch-phrase is "sign on the dotted line!" Somehow he manages to impress Amy Fisher (Madge Evans), the girl he met on an excursion boat. She accepts his marriage proposal, much to the consternation of her exasperated family, which sees through his delusions of grandeur.

Due to Aubrey's extravagance, the couple live beyond their means. Soon Aubrey's sala-

BOTTOMS UP (1934). With Herbert Mundin, Pat Paterson, and Sid Silvers

ry is attached and he and Amy are forced to move in with her folks. Then Aubrey is fired after causing his company to buy worthless land. On top of this, his interference prevents his brother-in-law from selling an invention. This is the last straw for Amy. She tells Aubrey to leave and "come back when you're a man."

In the end, accidental good fortune puts everything right. The land turns out to be valuable, and the invention is sold at a much higher price. Aubrey gets his job back and is his old overbearing self again. By this time, Amy and her family are resigned to their fate.

Tracy made five more films for Fox before his contract was terminated by mutual agreement.

Nineteen thirty-four was a banner year for musicals, and *Bottoms Up* was one of the better ones. Song-and-dance numbers were subordinated to the story, which was a satire on Hollywood. Tracy had another of the fast-talking, wisecracking roles he did so well. The picture also introduced Pat Paterson, a new British actress, who played a Canadian beauty-contest winner trying to break into the movies. Her money runs out, but she is befriended by Tracy, Herbert Mundin, and Sid Silvers—three out-of-work men who take her to live with them in an abandoned hut on a miniature golf course. Tracy is a down-on-his-luck press

55

NOW I'LL TELL (1934). With Alice Faye

agent, Mundin a forger recently out of jail, and Silvers an ex-jockey.

Tracy cooks up a phony publicity campaign to launch Paterson on a screen career. He has her pretend to be the daughter of an English nobleman, impersonated by Mundin. Tracy then engineers a "romance" between the girl and an alcoholic film star (John Boles). This leads to a part in one of Boles's pictures. Naturally, she is a great success. When Tracy realizes that Paterson and Boles are truly in love, he suppresses his own feelings and gallantly steps aside.

Bottoms Up was not nearly as spectacular as some of the Warners and MGM extravaganzas of the period, but it did have tuneful songs, a bright and witty script, and an ingratiating cast. Two lilting ballads—"Little Did I Dream" and "Waiting at the Gate for Katie"—were nicely rendered by Boles. Tracy did not sing. He had to wait a few years for that opportunity.

Now I'll Tell was based on a book by Carolyn Rothstein, the wife of notorious gambler Arnold Rothstein. Rothstein's murder in 1928 had provided the material for several earlier films, most notably *The Street of Chance* (1930), starring William Powell. But *Now I'll Tell* was supposed to be the definitive version of the events leading up to his death.

The names of the principal characters were changed to Murray and Virginia. Golden. Although some aspects of the film resembled a "true-confessions" soap opera, writer-director Edwin Burke delivered, for the most part, a sober, straightforward story about a big-time gambler's downfall. Once again, Tracy portrayed a man destroyed by his desire for wealth and power. His interesting, sharply defined performance lifted the picture out of the familiar rut of underworld melodrama and turned it into another absorbing character study. Tracy's Murray Golden was a shrewd, crafty manipulator, but also recognizably human with many good traits. Tracy received solo star billing; Fox also gave him a well-mounted production and strong support from Helen Twelvetrees as the wife and newcomer Alice Faye, surprisingly effective in the dramatic role of Golden's ill-fated mistress. Briefly seen in one episode was five-year-old Shirley Temple, playing the daughter of one of Golden's associates.

Now I'll Tell was a star vehicle for Tracy, but *Marie Galante*, his followup film was specifically designed to introduce another new European actress, the French-born Ketti Gallian. *Marie Galante* was based on a novel and play by Jacques Deval. Deval's original heroine, a tragic prostitute who meets an untimely end, underwent extensive revisions in the screen translation. Fox made her an innocent girl— a café singer stranded in the Panama Canal zone—who gets caught up in an international plot to blow up the canal. Tracy was a US intelligence officer, posing as a scientist, who exposes the conspiracy in time to prevent the sabotage, unmasks the super criminal behind the plot, and wins the girl.

Marie Galante did not enhance the short-lived Hollywood career of Ketti Gallian—she appeared in only three more films —and Tracy was clearly wasted. The legendary Helen Morgan added a little distinction to the proceedings in the small role of a café proprietress. She sang two songs in her inimitable style.

The pretentious *Dante's Inferno* is the most elaborate of Tracy's Fox features. The studio had made a silent picture with that title in 1924, but Tracy's vehicle is not a remake, although it did contain an allegorical se-

DANTE'S INFERNO (1935). With Claire Trevor.

quence of souls burning in hell that was similar to scenes in the earlier film. The 1935 *Dante's Inferno* also featured a climactic fire aboard a luxury liner. These two spectacular episodes helped make the film a financial success in its initial release and subsequent reissues.

Dante's Inferno cast Tracy in still another variation of his now-standard role—an unscrupulous opportunist who rises to power and wealth, and then loses all. Here, at least, he is given the opportunity to learn the error of his ways and reform. Tracy is an ex-stoker determined to shape his life along the lines of Alexander the Great. Starting as a highly aggressive carnival barker, he makes a fortune buying up amusement piers and creating elaborate attractions such as "Dante's Inferno." Later he is brought to trial for ignoring safety measures that resulted in the collapse of one of the piers. He lies his way out of the charges and next invests in a luxurious gambling ship, which is destroyed by fire. His quick thinking saves the lives of all the passengers, including his small son. Now completely wiped out, he is forgiven for his past misdeeds by his estranged wife (Claire Trevor), and they start a new life together.

The trite story did have the benefit of colorful carnival atmosphere, imaginative sets—the amusement park had an oddly surrealistic appearance—and generally good acting, especially by Henry B. Walthall as an old-

IT'S A SMALL WORLD (1935). With Raymond Walburn and Virginia Sale

time carnival man who takes Tracy's "Inferno" attraction all too seriously. Rita Hayworth, under the name of Rita Cansino, made her screen debut in a dancing bit.

It's a Small World, Tracy's last film for Fox, was released before *Dante's Inferno*. Critics dismissed it as a half-baked imitation of *It Happened One Night* and a low point in his career. The film introduced British actress Wendy Barrie to Hollywood as one of those dizzy debutantes inspired by Claudette Colbert's Ellie Andrews. Taking off in her car with no destination in mind, she becomes farcically and romantically involved with a lawyer (Tracy). They run into all sorts of eccentric rural types, including a zany judge (Raymond Walburn) who has them arrested for disturbing the peace. (Actually, he only wants to promote their romance.)

Tracy threatened to quit if Fox put him in more trivial romantic comedies like *It's a Small World*. He took a firm stand after the studio assigned him to a supporting role in *The Farmer Takes a Wife*, with Janet Gaynor and Henry Fonda, a new young actor who would repeat his stage role. On April 8, 1935, Tracy obtained his release. The same day, he signed a new contract with MGM, where he would remain for the next twenty years.

He had completed his apprenticeship, dutifully playing a variety of aggressive and sometimes soft-hearted men in mostly mediocre films. Now he was ready to mellow and deepen his image, to create the sure and steady Spencer Tracy that film audiences would remember.

Top MGM executives Irving Thalberg and Louis B. Mayer disagreed about Tracy's qualifications for stardom. Thalberg was certain that Tracy, by sheer acting ability alone, would be an important addition to the studio's impressive list of contract players. Mayer felt he lacked the necessary charisma, and decided to test his sex appeal by pairing him with a few of the more glamorous leading ladies.

MGM rushed Tracy through three pictures in 1935. They were expertly produced, but otherwise lacked distinction. They did, however, offer some variety. The first, *Murder Man*, is an offbeat, thickly plotted yarn about a newspaper reporter out to avenge his wife's suicide. The revenge motive and the brooding central character, vividly realized in Tracy's arresting low-key performance, bear a passing resemblance to the later *Fury*. Tracy murders a crooked stockbroker responsible for the death of his wife, convinces the police that the dead man's partner is guilty, comes to his senses, and confesses all before the accused goes to the chair. The film was minor melodrama but Tracy was impressive, especially in his scenes at a shooting gallery, where he enjoyed his favorite pastime. Virginia Bruce and James Stewart

THE MGM PERIOD (1935-1955)

(in his screen debut) provided good support as two other reporters.

Riffraff reunited Tracy with Jean Harlow. In the four years since *Goldie*, the actress had become one of the decade's most vivid screen personalities. Already a reigning sex symbol, she also achieved recognition as a deft, brashly funny comedienne. Harlow had been less effective in several dramatic parts, but producer Thalberg was determined to prove with *Riffraff* that she could handle serious roles. Harlow and Tracy made a striking team as two tough, boisterous waterfront types. Their rowdy love scenes early in the film are alternately comic and touching. But the topheavy script worked against them. Overloaded with subordinate characters and a contrived storyline that barely makes sense, *Riffraff* failed to provide a fitting showcase for its stars. (The best performance is given by Joseph Calleia as a Greek tuna tycoon.)

Harlow, no longer platinum-haired and sporting a new, more natural blonde look, plays a can-

MURDER MAN (1935). With Lionel Atwill, Virginia Bruce, and William Collier, Sr.

nery worker who marries hot-headed fisherman Tracy. He is forced out of the union for instigating a strike, and leaves Harlow to become a hobo. After stealing money to help him, she lands in jail, where her baby is born. She escapes from prison for a stormy reunion with a repentant Tracy, before returning to serve out her jail sentence.

There is pungent thirties-style repartee in the early scenes. Following an argument, Harlow snubs Tracy at a dance. "Why waste time with this riffraff?" she tells her employer. "Look what's calling me riffraff," retorts Tracy, "a cheap little tuna dinner trying to red-apple the boss." But a short time later, they are dancing cheek to cheek.

Tracy: "You know, this ain't hard to take." Harlow: "Just coming to life, huh?" Tracy: "Oh, you little mule, keep it up. I love dames with spirit. Dames and fishes." Tracy proposes marriage after winning in a crap game. "I want to marry you because you spit lucky," he says. Harlow is properly indignant. "What do you think I am, just an old rabbit's foot to bring you luck?" Harlow's sarcastic sister (Una Merkel) frowns on the wedding. In her opinion, Tracy "has a heart like a harpoon."

Tracy started work on *Whipsaw* three days after completing *Riffraff*. *Whipsaw* cast him opposite Myrna Loy, another of MGM's rising stars. This slick cops-and-robbers tale followed a familiar chase pattern. However, the movie is made more intriguing by the romantic cat-and-mouse game played by Tracy and Loy throughout the film, which is strewn with minor incidents to embellish the basically thin plot. Tracy, a G-man on the trail of jewel thieves, tracks down gang member Loy, who is traveling cross-country with the gems. Tracy pretends to be a crook himself, so she will lead him to the others. There is the usual climactic shootout, complicated by the arrival of a second gang, also after the jewels. Loy, regenerated by love, helps Tracy bring all the criminals to justice.

Tracy's next three films for MGM, filmed in 1936, were a marked improvement: all major productions that have retained their popularity and stature over the years. And the popular and critical acclaim Tracy received for his performances catapulted him to stardom—a position that had eluded him for five years.

RIFFRAFF (1935). With J. Farrell MacDonald and Jean Harlow

WHIPSAW (1935). With Myrna Loy

San Francisco was the first to go into production. This spectacular tale of the Barbary Coast, climaxed by a startlingly realistic depiction of the 1906 earthquake, would have been MGM's most elaborate picture of the year if the studio had not also been making *The Great Ziegfeld* simultaneously. *San Francisco* was an enormous success and a triumph for everyone connected with its production. The two leading players, Clark Gable and Jeanette MacDonald, had roles that suited them perfectly, but it was Tracy, in the important supporting part of a rugged, understanding priest, who won the best notices and almost stole the film. He also received his first Academy Award nomination for Best Actor.

Tracy was at first reluctant to accept such a small role, and he also had some qualms about playing a priest. But director W. S. Van Dyke II, convinced that

Tracy was the only actor at MGM who could supply the necessary combination of humanity and virility, persuaded him to take the part.

San Francisco begins on New Year's Eve of 1906 and ends with the April 18 earthquake. In between, it packs a surprising amount of plot centering on Blackie Norton (Gable), the rough-hewn owner of a popular Barbary Coast café, and Mary Blake (MacDonald), the demure small-town minister's daughter who becomes a singer in his café. Blackie's lifelong friend is Father Tim Mullin (Tracy), who runs a nearby mission and church. From Father Tim, Mary learns all about Blackie, who both fascinates and frightens her. "He's as unscrupulous with women as he is ruthless with men," he tells her. "You probably understand Blackie a lot better than he understands you. Blackie never knew your type of woman before." The priest also warns Mary about San Francisco in an obviously prescient speech: "You're probably in the wickedest, most corrupt, most godless city in America. Sometimes it frightens me. I wonder what the end is going to be."

The romance of Blackie and Mary ends when she realizes he has no intention of marrying her,

Thirties portrait

and she leaves him to become a successful opera singer under the sponsorship of Blackie's rival, Burley (Jack Holt). Blackie tries to lure Mary back with a marriage proposal, but only precipitates a bitter fight with Burley. It takes an earthquake (a justly famous sequence notable for its brilliant special effects) to bring about Blackie's change of character. Wandering about the ruined city, looking for Mary, he finds Mullin caring for the injured in a makeshift hospital. Blackie and Mary are reunited on a hill overlooking the city as people gather

SAN FRANCISCO (1936). With Jeanette MacDonald

SAN FRANCISCO (1936). With Clark Gable, Jack Holt, and
Jeanette MacDonald

to rebuild the destroyed metropolis.

After completing his scenes in *San Francisco*, Tracy went right into *Fury*, which had already started production. Tracy gave one of his finest performances in this exceptionally powerful film, which was German director Fritz Lang's first American effort. Lang also worked on the screenplay with Bartlett Cormack from an original story by Norman Krasna. *Fury* was released several weeks before *San Francisco*, and on the strength of these two consecutive successes in disparate roles, Tracy was being hailed by critics as the actor of the year.

Fury was an unusually bold picture for MGM to make at this time. Nothing quite like it had been seen on the screen before. There are weaknesses. The second half of the film seems overly contrived and is not helped by a trite happy ending. But Lang's directorial skill and Tracy's intense acting obscure some of the defects.

Fury is a terrifying study of mob violence photographed in the harsh gray tones Lang had used in *M*, and other of his German films. Tracy played Joe Wheeler, a happy, honest, hardworking young man passing through a small midwestern town. He is falsely arrested on a kidnapping-murder charge and jailed as a suspect. "Am I the only guy in the world that eats peanuts?" he asks at the police station when confronted with the circumstantial evidence against him. Hysterical townspeople try to lynch him and, failing in this, set fire to the jail. Tracy is seen from his cell window shouting his innocence. Then the building is dynamited as Tracy's sweetheart (Sylvia Sidney) watches from the distance in horror.

A short time later the real criminal is apprehended, and Tracy secretly "returns from the dead." He managed to escape from the prison and is now a bitter, warped man seeking revenge. He convinces his two brothers that the mob's leaders should be brought to trial for his "murder." He explains his feelings to them in a speech delivered with searing force by Tracy: "Do you know where I've been all day? In a movie watching a newsreel of myself gettin' burned alive. Watched it ten or twenty times maybe. Over and over again. The place was packed. They like it. They get a big kick out of seeing a man burned to death. What an explosion! It blew the cell door off. I got down a rainpipe. I almost burned my side off. I could smell

FURY (1936). As Joe Wheeler

68

myself burn. But that don't hurt me 'cause you can't hurt a dead man and I'm dead. I'm burned to death by a mob of animals. I'm legally dead and they're legally murderers. That I'm alive is not their fault. But I know 'em. I know lots of 'em. And they'll hang for it. According to the law which says if you kill somebody you got to be killed yourself. But I'll give them the chance they didn't give me. They'll get a legal trial in a legal courtroom. They'll have a legal judge and a legal defense. They'll get a legal sentence and a legal death."

Twenty-two members of the mob go on trial with the newsreel footage used as evidence of their guilt. Sidney finally persuades Tracy to come out of hiding. He makes a dramatic appearance in court and saves the lives of the accused citizens. He addresses the judge with these words: "I know that by coming here I've saved these people. But that isn't why I'm here. I don't care anything about saving them. The law doesn't know that a lot of things that were important to me, silly things maybe, like a belief in justice, and an idea that men were civilized, and a feeling of pride that this country of mine was different from all others. The law doesn't know that these things

were burned to death within me that night."

Tracy switched from grim melodrama to light comedy in his next picture, and did it with effortless ease. *Libeled Lady* (1936) was one of the funniest of the romantic screwball comedies so popular at the time. Jean Harlow, William Powell, and Myrna Loy were billed over Tracy, but the four roles were more or less equal and he more than held his own as a glib newspaper editor involved in a libel suit. Jack Conway directed at a merry clip, and the script was generously endowed with bright lines and amusing situations.

At the beginning of the film, Tracy is dressing for his own formal wedding. "Here's to the last mile," he says to his reflection in the mirror as he swills down a drink. He is suddenly called to the office because his paper is being sued for five million dollars. His fiancée (Harlow), who had been left waiting at the church, comes flouncing in, still wearing her bridal gown, to tell Tracy what she thinks of him. Then the fun really starts.

The paper has printed an untrue story linking heiress Loy romantically with a married man. Tracy devises a scheme that will implicate Loy in a real scandal and thus prevent her

LIBELED LADY (1936). With William Powell and Jean Harlow

from suing. To accomplish this, he hires Powell, a suave lawyer and ladies' man, temporarily in need of funds. Tracy talks an infuriated Harlow into a marriage in name only with Powell. The wedding scene contains a well-remembered comic moment. After the ceremony, Harlow gives Powell a perfunctory kiss and then goes into a passionate embrace with Tracy. "He's a good friend," Powell explains to the astonished minister. "A *very* good friend."

Powell then attempts to win Loy's affections. She is wary at first, but they soon fall genuinely in love. Feeling neglected by Tracy, Harlow complicates mat-

ters by becoming infatuated with Powell. She taunts Tracy with remarks like: "You'd make your crippled grandmother do a fan dance for that paper." Harlow's new indifference disturbs Tracy. "She may be his wife, but she's engaged to me," he tells a friend. In the end, the four principals gather for a final showdown, some surprising revelations, and the inevitable pairing-off of the right couples.

Harlow and Tracy's teamwork delighted audiences. Two subsequent films planned as co-starring vehicles were abandoned after Miss Harlow's death the following year.

Early in 1937, Tracy appeared in *Captains Courageous*, one of his finest films during the decade, and an MGM achievement of universal appeal. This adaptation of Rudyard Kipling's novel is not completely faithful to the book. The principal change is in the character played by Tracy. Manuel, the mystical Portugese fisherman, became the second lead instead of a lesser figure.

The precocious child actor Freddie Bartholomew played Harvey, the spoiled twelve-year-old son of a wealthy businessman (Melvyn Douglas). At school, Harvey lies, cheats, browbeats classmates, and even threatens teachers. He is expelled and taken on an ocean voyage by his father. He falls off the ship near the Grand Banks and is rescued by Manuel, who takes him aboard the schooner *We're Here*. The rest of the crew have no use for the rebellious Harvey, but Manuel is drawn to the boy he calls "leetle feesh."

Manuel is outwardly boisterous and happy-go-lucky, but there is also a religious side to him and he has a poetic nature. He likes to sing and play the vielle, a musical instrument handed down from his father. "I don't write songs," Manuel tells Harvey. "I just find them in my mouth. Say, sometimes a song is

CAPTAINS COURAGEOUS (1937).
As Manuel

71

CAPTAINS COURAGEOUS (1937). With Lionel Barrymore and Freddie Bartholomew

so big and sweet inside, I just can't get him out, and then I look up at the stars and maybe cry and feel so good."

Harvey gradually responds to Manuel's kindness and a warm friendship develops between them. The fisherman's simple philosophy of life inspires Harvey to learn discipline and a sense of honor and fair play. Soon he is accepted as a regular member of the crew.

Manuel is killed during a storm at sea. A heartbroken Harvey returns, a completely different person, to his father. As he talks about his exciting adventures, his thoughts are with his dead friend. The last shot of the film is a superimposed closeup of Manuel.

Skillfully directed by Victor Fleming, *Captains Courageous* was one of the year's outstanding films. Tracy's gentle, deeply felt performance, totally unlike anything he had done before, won for him his first Academy Award. Yet it was not a role he particularly wanted to play, even though he liked the script. He felt he was all wrong for it from the beginning, despite the encouragement of his wife and Fleming. But he allowed his hair to be curled, worked hard on a Portuguese accent, and somehow managed to sing two sea chanteys written especially for him.

In time, Tracy listed *Captains Courageous* as one of his personal favorites, but he suffered during the filming of the picture. He said: "I used to pray that something would happen to halt production. I was positive I was doing the worst job of my life. I just felt sure I couldn't surmount the singing and the dialect, and the curled hair. If anyone had predicted that the part would win an Academy Award when I was working before the cameras I'd have thought he was delirious."

They Gave Him a Gun (1937), Tracy's next picture, was a curious mixture of sentimentality, preachment against war, and underworld melodrama. An uneven and disappointing film, it was helped by the excellent performances of Tracy, Gladys George, and Franchot Tone under W. S. Van Dyke's direction. There were several good battle scenes in the first half of the movie. However, its story of two war buddies who share different fates but love the same woman was frayed material. (The war turns Tone into a hardened criminal, and Tracy becomes the manager of a traveling circus who shelters and finally wins Gladys George.)

Tracy made two films in a

THEY GAVE HIM A GUN (1937). With Franchot Tone

BIG CITY (1937). With Luise Rainer

row with his old friend Frank Borzage, recently put under contract by MGM. In *Big City* (1937), he was costarred with Viennese actress Luise Rainer, then at the peak of her fame. This contrived story about a cabdriver involved in a taxi war and his immigrant wife did little to enhance the reputation of either star. Tracy was up against an outfit who used gangster methods to fight independent cabbies like himself. For novelty value, the picture featured cameo appearances by such famous boxers as Jack Dempsey, James J. Jeffries, Jim Thorpe, Man Mountain Dean, and Maxie Rosenbloom, all playing themselves.

They help Tracy and his friends defeat the hoodlums in a rousing finale. (Released again the following year, the film did better-than-average business because both Tracy and Rainer were Oscar winners by then.)

Mannequin (1938), his second MGM film with Borzage, is strictly a Joan Crawford soap opera, typical of her vehicles and adhering to the standard formula of Crawford torn between two men. She played a slum girl who survives an unfortunate marriage to a petty crook (Alan Curtis) and becomes a top model. Tracy lent sturdy support as a wealthy, self-made businessman from her old neighborhood. He marries

Crawford on the rebound. Of course, the first husband tries to make trouble for them. When Tracy loses his fortune, Crawford comes to his rescue with her jewel box and thereby proves her love for him.

Films like *Mannequin* didn't help Tracy's morale, especially after his success in *Captains Courageous*. Nor was he particularly happy about *Test Pilot* (1938), which was a tremendously popular aerial film about the strains and pressures of a dangerous profession. He played second fiddle to Clark Gable and Myrna Loy, although his role was built up to match theirs. Gable is a daredevil pilot,

and Tracy his mechanic and close friend. Loy played a Kansas girl who marries Gable only twenty-four hours after he has made a forced landing on her father's farm.

Tracy's character is established early in the film. He watches over Gable like a loyal big brother. Every time Gable tests a plane, Tracy sticks his chewing gum on it for good luck, but he knows the score. ("It's death every time you move.") When Gable gets drunk, Tracy is always around to put him to bed and chase the girls away. Tracy does not take kindly to the unexpected bride at first, but after a while the three are inseparable—

TEST PILOT (1938). With Myrna Loy and Clark Gable

MANNEQUIN (1938). With Joan Crawford.

that is, until Gable's drinking gets out of hand and Loy starts to fall apart. Tracy is a glumly silent witness to the quarrels and reconciliations.

Gable tests a new plane for the Army, with Tracy as his co-pilot. This time, Tracy spits the gum out of his mouth. "Okay, pal, last flight," he tells Gable. Up in the air, the ropes holding the sandbags break, and Tracy is crushed under the weight. The plane crashes and Gable pulls his dying friend out of the blaze. "I won't ever have to go home to break the news to her," Tracy whispers to Gable. "Don't die, for my sake," Gable pleads. "That's all I'd come back for if I could" are Tracy's final words.

Tracy's death convinces Gable he should switch to ground work for Loy's sake. Now he is the one sticking gum on the tails of planes about to take off.

Tracy received the customary critical praise for *Test Pilot*. But he let it be known that he wouldn't be partial to a steady diet of Gable-Tracy films, although personally he was quite fond of his costar.

Tracy gave a truly inspired performance in *Boys Town*, his third 1938 film. He impersonated Father Edward J. Flanagan, the dedicated Catholic priest who established a school and community for homeless boys in Nebraska. The central character and basic situations were real, but the film suffers from an overdose of syrupy sentimentality and hackneyed melodramatic situations. Despite the cliché-ridden fictional portions of the script, Tracy managed a characterization that can only be called ideal.

As in the past, he had trepidations about the role before filming began. He later said: "I knew Father Flanagan personally, and felt nobody could put over his warmth, inspiration, and humaneness of feeling in a picture. But I became so absorbed in the part that by the end of the first week I had stopped worrying."

The first half of the picture is far superior to the second, which has aspects of a grade-B crime thriller. In Tracy's first scene, there are hints that he might be attempting an Irish brogue, but this is happily abandoned for a straightforward delivery of lines. He visits a condemned convict (Leslie Fenton) in his prison cell. The convict tells the priest that if he had had one good friend as a child, he wouldn't have gone wrong.

Father Flanagan's belief that "there's no such thing in the world as a bad boy" gives him

BOYS TOWN (1938). With Mickey Rooney

the incentive to start his first home for underprivileged youngsters, with the financial assistance of a skeptical pawnbroker friend (Henry Hull). Soon he is housing more boys than he can handle. In a touching Christmas Eve scene, Flanagan admits that he can't even afford a tree, but the pawnbroker pays a surprise visit with gifts for everyone. Later, contributions pour in and the buildings making up Boys Town are constructed.

Enter Mickey Rooney as a tough teenage hoodlum named Whitey Marsh. His older brother, about to go to prison, has given Flanagan money to look after him. Predictably, Whitey refuses to submit to discipline and clashes with the other boys, finally running away from Boys Town. He seems to be the only kid Flanagan has been unable to reach. But later Whitey redeems himself by helping Flanagan and the boys capture a gang of bank robbers. Whitey becomes a model citizen and is elected mayor of Boys Town.

Tracy's quiet dignity is even more impressive in contrast to Rooney's brash mugging. Much of the film was shot at the Nebraska community. Made on a modest budget, *Boys Town*'s success exceeded all expectations.

Accepting 1938 Academy Award with Bette Davis (Best Actress).
Giving the award: Sir Cedric Hardwicke

Tracy won his second Academy Award for his portrayal of Father Flanagan, making him the only actor ever to win an Oscar two years in succession. He gave his award to Flanagan with an added inscription: "To Father Edward J. Flanagan, whose great human qualities, kindly simplicity and inspiring courage were strong enough to shine through my humble efforts."

A screen version of Kenneth Roberts's best-selling historical novel *Northwest Passage* was announced as Tracy's next picture, but there were script problems and MGM postponed production. Louis B. Mayer decided to cast Tracy opposite Hedy Lamarr in *I Take This Woman*, based on an original story by Charles MacArthur. Mayer was certain that Lamarr, his latest European discovery, would be as great a star as Greta Garbo and Marlene Dietrich. And the Viennese beauty had created a sensation when Mayer loaned her out to Walter Wanger for *Algiers*. Mayer hired Josef von Sternberg, the man who made Dietrich famous, to direct *I Take This Woman*.

The film went before the cameras in January 1939. Von Sternberg resigned after Mayer refused to allow any script changes. The director was replaced by Frank Borzage. The picture was nearing completion when the studio chose to shelve it and begin again with still another director and an entirely different supporting cast. Only Tracy and Lamarr would be retained, but Tracy had been promised to 20th Century-Fox for *Stanley and Livingstone*, which was ready to start shooting. *I Take This Woman* shut down indefinitely and Tracy reported for work at his old studio, which had since merged with Darryl F. Zanuck's 20th Century Pictures.

Stanley and Livingstone (1939), an historical drama based on fact, was a superior film and another triumph for Tracy. He played *The New York Herald* reporter Henry M. Stanley, who went to Africa to search for the lost missionary Dr. David Livingstone (Sir Cedric Hardwicke). Stanley eventually finds Livingstone, whom many believed dead, working among the natives in an isolated village. He returns to civilization to bring news of the dedicated doctor's achievements in medical research. Only a few believe him and attempts are made to discredit Stanley as a

STANLEY AND LIVINGSTONE (1939). With Walter Brennan

I TAKE THIS WOMAN (1940). With Hedy Lamarr

lying opportunist. But news that Livingstone has just died arrives in time to exonerate Stanley, and the newspaperman is able to prove that all his statements are true. Stanley then returns to Africa to continue Livingstone's work.

The dramatic highlight of the film is Tracy's long, impassioned speech to his detractors at a legal hearing, which he delivered magnificently. Some fictional characters were written into the script, including a girl (Nancy Kelly) whom Stanley loves but loses to a younger suitor. The famous first meeting between the title characters, in which Tracy utters the celebrated line—"Dr. Livingstone, I presume?"—was filmed with commendable restraint.

Tracy went back to MGM to resume work on *I Take This Woman* (1940), this time with W. S. Van Dyke II directing. The lavishly mounted soap opera proved to be execrable when it was finally released early in 1940, hardly worth all the trouble involved. The story had Tracy, as a doctor, rescue a café-society playgirl from suicide. They marry, and Tracy gives up his tenement district clinic for private practice in order to provide the kind of life she is accustomed to. He leaves her when he thinks she is contemplating infidelity, but she proves her love and they return to his old clinic together. It was a dreary romantic drama not even Tracy's sincerity could save.

Several scriptwriters had been unable to solve the multiple problems of adapting *Northwest Passage* into a suitable screenplay. Only the first half of the script was ready for filming. MGM instructed director King Vidor to start production on this ambitious project while Laurence Stallings and Talbot Jennings attempted to complete a final shooting script. The company went to Oregon for extensive location work.

Tracy had the role of Major Robert Rogers, leader of Rogers' Rangers, who led his men on a perilous expedition to defeat a murderous Indian tribe in 1759, during the French and Indian Wars. This portion of the story was completed after twelve arduous weeks of filming in wilderness country under extremely difficult conditions. When Vidor ran out of script, he was told to wrap up production. The second half of the novel had been abandoned. Only the completed foot-

NORTHWEST PASSAGE (1940). With Robert Young

EDISON THE MAN (1940). As Thomas Alva Edison

age would be released, with a brief prologue and epilogue to be added later. The film ends with Rogers preparing for a new trek —his search for the Northwest Passage—which was to have been the major part of the movie.

The picture, as released, was nevertheless immensely popular. The public flocked to this rousing adventure story, although some viewers were reportedly put off by the scene in which a crazed ranger insists on hoarding the head of one of his Indian victims. *Northwest Passage* was, incidentally, the first color movie for both Tracy and Vidor.

Tracy's next assignment, *Edison the Man,* was one that he was particularly proud to handle. Actually the second part of MGM's tribute to the American inventor, it followed *Young Tom Edison* into theaters. The earlier film, with Mickey Rooney in the title role, covered Edison's boyhood years. Tracy portrayed Edison from the ages of twenty-five to eighty-two. He considered the role to be his most demanding to date. He later told an interviewer: "I gradually worked out of my feeling of being afraid I wouldn't do everything that the character merited and just went ahead from day to day, trying my best. I lived in the Edison at-

mosphere as much as I could for a couple of months ahead of production. In these days, when you run into some kind of 'ism' everywhere you turn, I think Edison's life is the best case history, in a dramatic form, American young people could possibly get on the things this country makes possible and stands for."

The film traces the inventor's career from the time he arrives in New York a penniless idealist to his successful experiments in electric lighting. Everything about the movie—period atmosphere, script and supporting cast, Clarence Brown's direction, Herbert Stothart's muted score—was first-rate, and the picture holds up beautifully today.

It begins with a prologue. The year is 1929. On the evening of Thomas A. Edison's Golden Jubilee Celebration, the aged man gives an interview to two high-school students before going to the banquet in his honor. Tracy's makeup is quite effective and he speaks his lines in a soft whisper that evokes a proper touch of gentle humor. He tells the awed youngsters that "one percent inspiration is very important. You cannot invent it. You have to have it."

At the banquet, Edison relives the main events of his life

EDISON THE MAN (1940). With Rita Johnson

during the salutory speeches. As a young man, he comes to New York from Boston, takes a menial job, meets his future wife (Rita Johnson) when he mends her umbrella, and sells a stock-tape machine invention to the Western Union Company. With the proceeds, he builds his laboratory at Menlo Park, where he produces the phonograph and perfects the first electric light bulb. Against strenuous opposition, he is given the opportunity to illuminate a New York City district if he can meet a six-month deadline. By much concentrated effort and work, he and his staff succeed.

Interspersed with the laboratory sequences are scenes of Edison at home, the birth of his two children, and his devoted wife's concern over his health. The picture ends with Edison once more listening to tributes at the 1929 testimonial dinner. "He would have been an important man even if he hadn't invented anything," says the toastmaster. Included in this speech is an ominous prediction about World War II and the possible future destruction of mankind. Edison gravely contemplates the words: "What man's mind can conceive, man's character can control."

Most critics agreed with Howard Barnes of *The New York Herald Tribune* when he wrote: "For almost any player except Tracy, the role would be thankless. Edison is shown as an irascible, stubborn, insatiably curious man whose personal existence was exceedingly mundane, and whose professional achievements defy dramatic projection. Nevertheless, by the sheer persuasion of his acting Tracy makes the film definitely worth seeing. It is a relief to find an actor relying on his own artifice, not grease paint, to bring a great figure to life. It is a completely credible portrayal."

Boom Town (1940) was Tracy's last cinematic fling with Clark Gable. Once again, MGM saddled Tracy with the role of a "good-natured goof who doesn't get the girl," while Gable divided his time between wife Claudette Colbert and mistress Hedy Lamarr. This flamboyant four-star special, MGM's biggest moneymaker of 1940, cast Gable and Tracy as two wildcat oil drillers who start out together with nothing. Tracy loses his fiancée (Colbert) to Gable but remains a loyal friend. Over the years, the two men quarrel, rec-

oncile, and make and lose millions in the oil industry. When business interests bring the partners to New York, Lamarr is introduced as a threat to Colbert's happiness. Tracy gallantly attempts to remove the obstacle by proposing marriage to Lamarr in a curt, decidedly unromantic fashion. "I'll buy you a diamond daybed for Christmas," he tells her. Lamarr, who knows Tracy's heart really belongs to Colbert, declines, but remarks candidly how lucky Colbert is to have the love of two prize men among men.

Gable and Tracy eventually engage in fisticuffs. Shortly thereafter, both men lose their fortunes. Gable is brought into court on an antitrust suit, but Tracy's testimony saves him from going to prison. The ending finds the two men friends again, back with Colbert in the oil fields where they began.

After *Boom Town*, which Tracy didn't want to do, he demanded and received top billing on all future pictures. MGM also promised him approval of vehicles and increased his salary.

Tracy agreed to do a sequel to *Boys Town* with Mickey Rooney, entitled *Men of Boys Town* (1941). Since Rooney was now one of MGM's most valuable properties, the studio anticipated

BOOM TOWN (1940). With Marion Martin and Clark Gable

BOOM TOWN (1940). With Claudette Colbert

MEN OF BOYS TOWN (1941). With Addison Richards, Henry O'Neill, Mary Nash, Mickey Rooney, and Darryl Hickman

another bonanza instead of the moderate success the picture turned out to be. This time out, Father Flanagan and Whitey Marsh, founder and junior mayor of the Nebraska community, expose brutal conditions in a reform school and also straighten out a couple of mixed-up kids along the way. The plot—again relying heavily on sentiment, broad comedy, and contrived melodrama—has Whitey adopted for a time by a wealthy family. But he cannot adjust to high life, and later he becomes innocently involved in a robbery charge, which lands him in the corrupt reformatory. Father Flanagan comes to the rescue, Whitey's former foster parents contribute badly needed financial support to Boys Town, and all is well.

Tracy's most important 1941 release was an expensive remake of the old horror thriller *Dr. Jekyll and Mr. Hyde*, which had served Fredric March so well a decade earlier. For virtually the first time in his career, Tracy received poor notices from the critics, who accused the actor of hamming it up too blatantly. But considering the material given him, Tracy turned in a respectable piece of work. His makeup as Hyde was not as horrifying as March's, but it was ghoulish enough, if somewhat too simian. Victor Fleming directed expertly, and Joseph Ruttenberg's fine photography evoked the proper menacing mood.

Sweden's Ingrid Bergman, whose progress had been slow during her first two years in Hollywood, scored an emphatic personal success as the terrified barmaid brutally victimized and murdered by Hyde. By contrast, Lana Turner was colorless and wooden in the nice-girl role.

Although it has been reported otherwise, Tracy certainly seemed to enjoy the challenge of this famous dual role. He had an actor's field day as the well-meaning doctor whose experiments to benefit the mentally disturbed caused him to become a homicidal fiend.

The picture made money, and Tracy liked working with Bergman. They subsequently costarred in a radio version of *Man's Castle*, one of Tracy's rare radio appearances.

In 1941, Tracy costarred for the first time with Katharine Hepburn, who was at the time riding the crest of renewed popularity following her triumph in the stage and screen versions of *The Philadelphia Story*. MGM had produced the film version of that play, and the studio was anxious to get Hepburn under contract. *Woman of the Year* was her pet project. She sold MGM both the script (an original by Ring Lardner, Jr., and Michael Kanin) and her services in a $211,000 package deal. And she chose the director, George Stevens, who had to be borrowed from RKO. Finally, she wanted Tracy for her leading man. She almost didn't get him. Tracy had started work on *The Yearling*, and was on location in Florida. Because of poor weather, production on *The Yearling* suddenly halted and the movie was temporarily shelved. Tracy never got to do this picture. When it was reactivated some years later, Gregory Peck played the lead.

Cancellation of *The Yearling* left Tracy free to do *Woman of the Year*. Hepburn was so pleased about it that she willingly agreed to take second billing.

Woman of the Year is an almost perfect romantic comedy, and it still retains its freshness and charm. Only a few incidental World War II aspects of the plot tend to date it slightly. It remains a pleasure to watch two seasoned professionals working together beautifully in a bright, witty screenplay, expertly tailored to their respective talents.

Tracy is a down-to-earth sports writer, and Hepburn an intellectual woman columnist on world affairs. They work for the same paper but haven't met. Their opposing attitudes toward war and baseball lead to some hostile remarks. It also leads to their first meeting in the office of the publisher who wants them to bury the hatchet. Tracy opens the door as Hepburn, sitting provocatively on top of a desk, is

DR. JEKYLL AND MR. HYDE (1941). As the evil Mr. Hyde

DR. JEKYLL AND MR. HYDE (1941). With Ingrid Bergman

WOMAN OF THE YEAR (1942). With Katharine Hepburn and Ludwig Stossel

straightening her stocking. There is a quick exchange of glances and it is apparent that these two are going to like each other. An immediate sexual attraction is subtly conveyed by the expressions on their faces. Sparks fly and the intangible quality generated by Tracy and Hepburn fairly lights up the screen. She accepts his request for a date, and so begins this warm, gently amusing account of two charming, disparate people drawn together and falling in love. They marry, but find themselves unable to adjust to their opposing personalities.

Their courtship begins with the first date. He takes her to a baseball game, where he answers Hepburn's excited and very ignorant questions about the game in relaxed, friendly tones. Later that evening, he arrives at her apartment with flowers, only to find himself out of place at a party of international celebrities.

entourage, she can only manage a few words to him. "Why did you ask me to come here?" he inquires as she is about to board the plane. "I thought you might want to kiss me goodbye," is her answer. And so, Tracy and Hepburn kiss for the first time on the screen.

Their second date takes place at Tracy's favorite bistro, where they talk about their past lives. In a taxi on their way to her apartment, he tells her he loves her. "Sure?" she asks. His reply: "Positive . . . even when I'm sober, even when you're brilliant." As their relationship de-

WOMAN OF THE YEAR (1942).
With Katharine Hepburn

Two men speaking English revert to a foreign language when he tries to join them. He sits next to a fat man from the Far East who can only say "Yes, Yes, Yes." Hepburn has no time at all for him, but the next day he finds a bottle of champagne on his desk with a note attached: "Sorry about last night."

Later, she asks him to accompany her to the airport. She is leaving for a personal-appearance tour. Surrounded by an

93

velops the two find a common ground of respect, admiration, and deepening affection. (At times the rapport between the two stars is miraculous to behold.) Finally, Tracy proposes marriage.

Because of her tight schedule, the wedding is a rushed affair in a small town. Their wedding night is interrupted by the unexpected arrival of European refugees. He decides to invite some of his old pals and their dates to the impromptu party, which creates more chaos and confusion. From then on, the marriage deteriorates steadily. They live in her cramped apartment, and the temporary adoption of a Greek orphan doesn't help matters. She is too busy to be any kind of a mother. Constant quarrels lead to a separation the night she accepts a "Woman of the Year" award at a banquet. Alone, she attends the wedding of her widowed father to the woman he has loved for years but never married. Hepburn realizes, while listening to the marriage vows, that she hasn't been a proper wife. A chastened Hepburn goes to Tracy's new bachelor quarters and she wins him back, despite her pathetic and hilarious attempts to prepare breakfast.

After the picture was completed, Tracy stated to an interviewer: "I was impressed with the legitimacy and honesty of the story. It's about understandable people and their problems, particularly the readjustment of a man and woman genuinely in love but poles apart in their outlook on life and marriage. Kate and I both tried to play our comedy scenes as simply as possible, and we had fun with them."

Woman of the Year, an unqualified success, marked the beginning of the famous Tracy-Hepburn partnership. It was also the start of a close and lasting personal relationship. Both gained a great deal from the friendship. Hepburn broadened his interests; he humanized hers.

By this time, Tracy was living alone in a hotel, but he kept in daily contact with his family and often spent weekends with them at the ranch.

Mrs. Tracy had her own life and work. Her son was finally able to speak after years of her instruction. In 1942, she founded the John Tracy Clinic at the University of Southern California. The clinic, which introduced new methods of training, taught families how to help deaf children, trained teachers for the deaf, and aided the afflicted children themselves. It all started in a small cottage on the USC

TORTILLA FLAT (1942). With Sheldon Leonard, Akim Tamiroff, and John Garfield

campus. Today, the clinic occupies a five-hundred-thousand-dollar building there and is considered the world's leading center in its field.

In his lifetime, Tracy gave much time and energy to raising money for the clinic. Without Tracy's financial and moral support, the clinic would not have been possible, according to Mrs. Tracy. During the first years, he alone kept it going and often spoke publicly on its behalf. Since it has always been a free clinic, Tracy contributed over half a million dollars to it, and also obtained, without asking,

sizable contributions from Walt Disney and many others. Mrs. Tracy has said her husband always had a "constant enthusiasm and interest in the clinic that were contagious." And Tracy once stated: "Nothing I've ever done can match what Louise has done for deaf children and their parents."

Mrs. Tracy seems to have been sympathetic about the Tracy-Hepburn association. She once remarked in an interview: "I have understood his restlessness and desire to lead his own life."

During World War II, Tracy

TORTILLA FLAT (1942). With Hedy Lamarr

occupied a unique position at MGM. Most of the male stars of the thirties had either left the studio or were in the armed forces. He was undisputedly top man among the actors. And MGM kept him busy. He also narrated two short films, written and directed by Garson Kanin, to aid the war effort.

For *Tortilla Flat* in 1942, Tracy attempted his first dialect role since *Captains Courageous*. In this adaptation of John Steinbeck's popular novel, he co-starred with Hedy Lamarr and John Garfield, and the picture was a reasonably faithful and entertaining transcription of the book. *Tortilla Flat* takes a semi-serious look into the lives of some poor Mexican peasants in a small Southern California seacoast town. Tracy is Pilon, the leader of a group of indolent, deceitful, but lovable *paisanos*, who are not above petty thievery. Pilon's friend Danny (Garfield) courts the village beauty Dolores (Lamarr). Pilon also has eyes for Dolores, and deliberately causes the two lovers to separate. Then he has a change of heart. He brings them together again, turning honest laborer to help provide some financial security for his friends. The acting was competent, but only Frank Morgan was outstanding as a religious-minded, dog-loving derelict.

Tortilla Flat was the fourth of five films Tracy made with director Victor Fleming. His next film, *Keeper of the Flame* (1942), his second with Hepburn, was also his first under George Cukor's direction. The film attempts to duplicate the style, mood, and atmosphere of Alfred Hitchcock's *Rebecca*, his 1940 prize-winning film. Similarities to the earlier movie include the story, which revolves around a dead person, and the setting—a dark, gloomy mansion that is also destroyed by fire. There are enigmatic characters and a somber, pervading air of mystery, but the picture lacks sufficient suspense. Nevertheless, it was intriguing and glossily produced in the best MGM manner. Furthermore, this psychological thriller provided Tracy and Hepburn with a change of pace from their earlier vehicle.

Tracy was a noted journalist investigating the "accidental" death, in an automobile, of a much revered US political figure. He suspects foul play and tries to get the true facts from the man's widow (Hepburn). The journalist is strongly attracted to this strange woman. She finally confesses to him that her husband was actually a sinister fascist who planned to overthrow the government. She could have prevented his death by warning him

KEEPER OF THE FLAME (1942). With Katharine Hepburn

A GUY NAMED JOE (1943). With Irene Dunne

of a defective bridge, but she allowed him to die so the world might remember him as a great man. Hepburn is killed by her husband's secretary (Richard Whorf), and Tracy is able to write the entire fantastic story.

Death also figured largely in Tracy's next film, *A Guy Named Joe* (1943), which paired him with Irene Dunne for the first and only time. The picture, directed by Victor Fleming, was an odd combination of romantic fantasy and aviation drama with a World War II background. MGM released the film as its 1943 Christmas attraction.

Although the critics had reservations about the film's merit, it found favor with audiences. *A Guy Named Joe* borrowed an idea from *Topper* and *Here Comes Mr. Jordan*, but played it for sentimental hokum rather than comedy. Tracy and Dunne are two pilots who are very much in love. They plan to marry, but Tracy is killed when his plane crashes into a Nazi carrier. He is allowed to return to earth unobserved by mortals, and helps the grief-stricken Dunne find happiness with another pilot (Van Johnson).

Johnson was a newcomer who soon became the idol of young movie fans. *A Guy Named Joe* did much to advance his career, but if it had not been for

A GUY NAMED JOE (1943). With Barry Nelson, Irene Dunne, Van Johnson, and Ward Bond

THE SEVENTH CROSS (1944). With Jessica Tandy and Hume Cronyn

Tracy's intervention he might not have achieved stardom. After production started, Johnson was seriously injured in a motor accident. MGM decided to replace him and reshoot his scenes with another actor. Tracy insisted that they shoot around Johnson until he recovered and was able to return to work. Esther Williams, another future star being groomed by MGM, appeared briefly in *A Guy Named Joe*.

Tracy obviously enjoyed his cheerful "ghost" role, and was his usual likable self. His love scenes with Miss Dunne had a charming sincerity that made the picture seem better than it really was. A highlight was Dunne's singing of the tender old ballad "I'll Get By (As Long As I Have You)." The title, incidentally, is figurative as there is no character in the movie named Joe.

Tracy was having trouble finding scripts that he liked, but he was sure he had a good one in *The Seventh Cross* (1944), a strong story set in pre-World War II Germany. Tracy's demanding role relied more on pantomime than dialogue. He may have been miscast, as some critics thought, but under the guidance of Fred Zinnemann, he came through with an intense, compelling performance in this taut, suspenseful chase film. *The Seventh Cross* gave Zinnemann his first major directorial opportunity. Tracy received solid support from an excellent cast, including Hume Cronyn, Signe Hasso, and Agnes Moorehead.

In *The Seventh Cross*, based on Anna Seghers's novel, Tracy plays an anti-Nazi German, one of seven inmates who escape from a concentration camp in 1936. The camp commandant has seven crosses placed in the yard. Six of the prisoners are captured and nailed to them. With the help of friends, Tracy survives the intensive hunt and makes his way to Holland.

MGM's ambitious 1944 production of *Thirty Seconds Over Tokyo* gave Van Johnson his first important starring role in a major dramatic picture. The film was based on Captain Ted W. Lawson's book about the Army Air Force raid on Tokyo led by Lieutenant Colonel James Doolittle. Tracy's participation in the picture as Doolittle was more in the nature of a guest appearance, since Johnson, playing Lawson, had a much larger part. Director Mervyn LeRoy convinced Tracy that he should take the role. He was the only actor, LeRoy pointed out, who could do justice to the famed Doolittle. Tracy did not make a mistake in accepting the assignment. He brought a note of distinction to one of the most memorable of all World War II films.

Without Love (1945), Tracy's third costarring venture with Hepburn, explored a lighter

THIRTY SECONDS OVER TOKYO (1944). With Van Johnson

WITHOUT LOVE (1945). With Katharine Hepburn

side of the war. This delightful romantic comedy was loosely based on a stage play by Philip Barry, which Hepburn had done on the stage. The much-altered screen version, released three years later, proved to be another agreeable frolic for the stars. Donald Ogden Stewart's script was a vast improvement over Barry's original.

The story, reminiscent of George Stevens's earlier *The More the Merrier,* makes use of the wartime Washington D.C. housing shortage for plot purposes. Tracy is a scientist who rents the home of a young widow (Hepburn) in order to conduct secret government experiments. They enter into a platonic marriage of convenience because he needs an assistant and she is willing to take the job. But he tends to walk in his sleep and she needs something (or someone) to warm her feet on cold nights. Inevitably, they fall in love.

It is not the flimsy storyline that matters here. The expert playing of the two stars clearly demonstrates that it is often possible to make something out of nothing with the help of a polished supporting cast (Keenan Wynn and Lucille Ball were especially funny) and a script-writer who knows how to write sparkling dialogue. *Without Love* revealed a maturing Tracy on the screen; his hair was definitely turning gray.

Tracy had a long-cherished ambition to return to the New York stage, and in 1945 he finally made it back to Broadway. He selected as his vehicle *The Rugged Path,* a play specially written for him by Robert E. Sherwood. His good friend Garson Kanin directed.

The drama had Tracy as a journalist serving as a cook on a Navy destroyer during World War II, and trying to find some meaning to a troubled world.

Tracy got fine personal notices after tryout performances in Providence and Washington D.C., but the play itself received a lukewarm critical reception. He seriously considered quitting the show more than once, but finally agreed to a limited Broadway engagement.

Tracy's return to the New York theater after an absense of fifteen years was a major event of the theatrical season. *The Rugged Path* opened on Broadway at the Plymouth on November 10, 1945. Critical reaction reflected the out-of-town opinions: raves for Tracy, disappointment in the play. Tracy's following insured sell-out business for eighty-one performances. Tracy refused to continue in it longer, and returned to Hollywood. He never appeared on the stage again.

No motion picture starring Tracy was released in 1946, but he spent a good part of the year filming *The Sea of Grass*, based on Conrad Richter's novel about a New Mexico cattle baron and his family in the 1880s. Tracy requested Katharine Hepburn for the feminine lead, and also approved of Elia Kazan as director. Kazan, still new to film direction—he had acted in a few early forties movies—had earned a brilliant reputation in the theater. He and Tracy did not get

WITHOUT LOVE (1945). With Katharine Hepburn

THE SEA OF GRASS (1947). With
Katharine Hepburn

along too well during production.

The Sea of Grass (1947) is essentially a lengthy soap opera in an Old West setting. The sprawling saga of an unhappy family spans many years. The two stars, aided by a large cast that included Melvyn Douglas, Harry Carey, and Phyllis Thaxter, strove valiantly to give it some meaning and life. Their individual characterizations are interesting, but the meandering script is against them all the way. Tracy had an unsympathetic role for a change, a ruthless land owner who bitterly opposes the new homesteaders. Hepburn is his neglected wife, unable to cope with her husband's obsessive nature. She bears two children—a daughter and son—the latter sired by another man. Tracy learns the truth, and Hepburn leaves him to face an uncertain future alone.

Years pass, and Tracy, unexpectedly, has grown to love his wife's bastard son (Robert Walker). But the boy is a wild one who gets into trouble with the law and is killed. Finally, Tracy and Hepburn are reunited by their daughter.

Unfortunately for Tracy, he chose to follow *The Sea of Grass* with another glorified soap opera, *Cass Timberlane* (1947), this time in modern dress. He had

THE SEA OF GRASS (1947). With Katharine Hepburn

CASS TIMBERLANE (1947). With Lana Turner

the title role in this slick drama based on a lesser Sinclair Lewis novel about a wealthy judge who marries a poor girl (Lana Turner) many years his junior. There are the usual complications caused by interfering friends from the judge's social set. Tracy suspects the innocent Turner of infidelity with Zachary Scott. He realizes his mistake after Turner suffers a near-fatal illness. The combined box-office lure of Tracy and Turner made *Cass Timberlane* a commercial success when it was released in late 1947, but the film was a hollow and tedious effort.

Tracy's luck changed the following year. Liberty Pictures, a newly established company bought the movie rights to Howard Lindsay and Russel Crouse's Pulitzer Prize-winning comedy *State of the Union*. Frank Capra, one of Liberty's founders, was going to direct the highly successful political satire. Tracy wanted to play the lead, so Louis B. Mayer arranged a deal with Capra. MGM would finance and distribute the film with Tracy and Claudette Colbert as costars. The picture was made at MGM and the studio supplied a capable supporting cast, which included Van Johnson, Angela Lansbury, Adolphe Menjou, and Lewis Stone. A dispute between Capra and Colbert resulted in the actress's withdrawal from the picture just as production was about to start. Katharine Hepburn took over the feminine lead on short notice, and delivered one of her most enchanting performances. At the time, she was just as much in need of a good picture as Tracy. Under Capra's firm direction, the team performed with all their old magic.

State of the Union is the type of film Capra did so well: the simple, upright man facing a den of crooks and thieves. Tracy had the role of an honest Presidential candidate who rebels against the corrupt politicians supporting him. He retains his integrity throughout a bitter campaign with the help of his loyal but estranged wife (Hepburn).

As Tracy grew older, finding suitable properties for him was not an easy task. His selection of *Edward, My Son* (1949) must be put down as a major career blunder. He seemed distinctly out of place in this turgid drama, adapted from a recent British stage play by Robert Morley and Noel Langley. Morley, a character actor of note, had also scored a hit on the London stage in the leading role. MGM produced the film in England. George Cukor directed, and a predominantly

STATE OF THE UNION (1948). With Katharine Hepburn

STATE OF THE UNION (1948). With Katharine Hepburn and Adolphe Menjou

British cast supported Tracy.

Edward, My Son, covering a twenty-year period, is the story of Arnold Boult (Tracy), who loves his only child obsessively and is determined to give the boy every advantage. To achieve this goal, he ruins the life of several people. His rise in the business world is accomplished through arson and the suicide of two associates. He takes a mistress and his wife becomes a hopeless alcoholic. Eventually, the beloved son turns out to be a wastrel who meets a bad end. Finally, Boult is sent to prison for his past misdeeds.

Donald Ogden Stewart's script made Tracy a Canadian, so the actor did not have to simulate a British accent. Otherwise,

the picture is generally faithful to the original. In neither play nor movie did the character of Edward ever appear. The film was made in the summer of 1948, but release was held up for almost a year. In the interim, Morley had triumphantly recreated his role on Broadway. The film and Tracy's performance suffered in comparison. Tracy received his worst set of notices since *Dr. Jekyll and Mr. Hyde*. Only Deborah Kerr survived the debacle. In fact, Miss Kerr's portrayal of the unfortunate wife won an Academy Award nomination. Leueen Mac-Grath, later Mrs. George S. Kaufman, who had played the mistress role with Morley on the stage, repeated the part in the

EDWARD, MY SON (1949). With James Donald

EDWARD, MY SON (1949). With Deborah Kerr

MALAYA (1950). As Carnahan

*MALAYA (1950). With James Stewart, Valentina Cortese,
and Sydney Greenstreet*

screen version.

While Tracy was filming in England, Dore Schary, once an MGM scriptwriter, had returned to that studio as "executive in charge of production," a position he formerly held at RKO. Schary submitted a script to Tracy—a World War II adventure story entitled *Operation Malaya*. Tracy reportedly accepted the lead because he liked the idea of doing a tough-guy part again. Another top star, James Stewart, agreed to costar with Tracy. They hadn't worked together since *Murder Man* in 1935. The unusually strong supporting cast listed such names as Sydney Greenstreet, John Hodiak, Lionel Barrymore, and Gilbert Roland. Italian actress Valentina Cortese was added to the male lineup to supply a bit of romance for Tracy as an old girlfriend he finds singing in a café.

Operation Malaya was based on a factual story, but what emerged on the screen was just another routine action yarn. Both Tracy and Stewart were wasted as two American soldiers of fortune who succeed in smuggling rubber out of Japanese-infested Malaya. Completed in late 1948, the film wasn't shown until January 1950, with its title shortened to *Malaya*.

By that time, Tracy had been seen in *Adam's Rib*, the only film he made in 1949. With this picture, Tracy and George Cukor more than made up for any ground lost on *Edward, My Son*. *Adam's Rib* is not only one of the best Tracy-Hepburn pictures, but possibly the best "battle-of-the-sexes" film comedy ever made. Garson Kanin and Ruth Gordon contributed a fresh, original, adult screenplay, ideally suited to the stars' talents and years ahead of its time. Cukor directed with wit and style, and the brilliant stage comedienne Judy Holliday gave a devastating comic performance that proved to be her stepping stone to stardom.

The picture opens with a clever parody of a typical crime of passion. A wife (Holliday) finds her husband and his paramour in their love nest, and shoots him. He is not killed, but the wife is brought to trial. She is prosecuted by Assistant District Attorney Adam Bonner (Tracy) and defended by Adam's lawyer-wife Amanda (Hepburn). Adam and Amanda share a happy marriage, their only failing an unfortunate penchant for calling each other "Pinky" and "Pinkie." But they take opposite sides on the subject of women's rights. Amanda does not believe in the single standard and her main argument

ADAM'S RIB (1949). With Katharine Hepburn

in court is sexual equality. As the trial progresses, the Bonners' conflicting theories disrupt their once tranquil home life. And David Wayne as Amanda's over-zealous admirer only adds fuel to the fire. Amanda wins the case and the accused is acquitted. By this time, the Bonner marriage is in serious trouble, but good old-fashioned common sense prevails and they talk themselves out of a separation.

Adam's Rib found Tracy and Hepburn in top form throughout this adroit satire. They brought such zest and hu-morous bite to the daily court-room antics and intimate eve-ning tete-à-tetes that it is impossible to imagine any other players in the rôles.

Father of the Bride (1950), another excellent comedy, re-vealed a stouter, frankly middle-aged Tracy, making no attempt to conceal his years. He made the transition to character roles gracefully. His hair had now turned completely gray.

Father of the Bride was based on a short novel by Ed-ward Streeter about an average American couple whose happy suburban home life is completely disrupted when their only daughter announces her engage-ment. From very slight material, Frances Goodrich and Albert Hackett fashioned a delightful screenplay, which Vincente Minnelli's direction and a perfect cast turned into a family picture full of humor and charm. The film was a great success with both critics and public, and Tracy's wise, warmly human performance in the title role earned him a fourth Academy Award nomination. Joan Bennett, reunited with Tracy for the first time in eighteen years, played the mother, and the part of the daughter was taken by Elizabeth Taylor, the seventeen-year-old former child actress soon to become one of the most popular stars of the new decade.

The story is told entirely from Tracy's viewpoint. As Stanley Banks, he addresses the audience directly at the beginning of the picture, and between dialogue scenes narrates the events leading up to the wedding. He is a lawyer of moderate income, and a loving husband and father, burdened with unexpected emotional adjustments and acute financial problems as preparations progress for a formal wedding. There are the initial meetings with his future son-in-law and the boy's parents, and painful encounters with caterers and decorators who take over his

ADAM'S RIB (1949). With Katharine Hepburn and Will Wright

FATHER OF THE BRIDE (1950). With Joan Bennett

FATHER OF THE BRIDE (1950). With Elizabeth Taylor

home. He survives the chaos and confusion of the wedding ceremony. and reception, and eventually finds solace in his daughter's happiness.

Tracy is the epitome of the much-put-upon father who must pay all the bills—alternately jealous, suspicious, protective, exasperated, and angry. His shrewd, knowing portrayal is all the more effective for its restraint.

Father of the Bride was so successful that MGM followed it with a sequel the next year. *Father's Little Dividend* (1951) had the same director and many of the players from the original film. In this movie, Tracy becomes a grandfather for the first time and must contend with the various additional adjustments

and problems involved. The picture did well, but Tracy turned down the idea of a possible series, which is what MGM had in mind.

The People Against O'Hara (1951) is not one of Tracy's major films, but he gave an interesting and moving performance as a once-brilliant criminal lawyer debilitated by alcoholism. He was also responsible for the casting of his old friend Pat O'Brien in a supporting role as a police detective. It was the first time the two had worked together in a film. O'Brien's career had not been going well and, principally to help him, Tracy consented to do the picture. It is the acting and John Sturges's competent direction that raise

FATHER'S LITTLE DIVIDEND (1951). With Moroni Olsen, Billie Burke, Joan Bennett, and Elizabeth Taylor

THE PEOPLE AGAINST O'HARA (1951). With Diana Lynn

The People Against O'Hara a notch above the level of an ordinary crime melodrama.

James Arness, later to become famous on television's *Gunsmoke*, played a young fish-market employee falsely accused of murder. Tracy comes out of retirement to defend him. Tracy is initially confident and assured, but the strains and pressures are too much for him and he begins to crack. He starts to drink again and loses the case. Tracy's subsequent detective work helps the police solve the murder, but he is killed bringing the real criminal to justice.

Pat and Mike (1952) placed Tracy on surer ground. He was happily reunited with Katharine Hepburn and the creative talents that had made *Adam's Rib* such an outstanding hit. Ruth Gordon and Garson Kanin came up with another smooth and clever script, and George Cukor's directorial flair was never more apparent. This rollicking satire on the sports world provided Tracy and

PAT AND MIKE (1952). With Charles Bronson, Katharine Hepburn, and George Mathews

PAT AND MIKE (1952). With Katharine Hepburn

PLYMOUTH ADVENTURE (1952). With Noel Drayton, Leo Genn, and Lowell Gilmore

PLYMOUTH ADVENTURE (1952). With Gene Tierney

Hepburn with roles that were quite different from anything they had done before.

Hepburn had a chance to display her considerable athletic prowess and also legs as beautiful as Dietrich's. She is Pat, a physical-education instructor at a college in California, who enters a national golf tournament. There she meets Mike (Tracy), a crude, uneducated, illiterate but genial promoter with his eye on an easy buck. He unsuccessfully attempts to bribe her into losing the game, but is impressed with her ability.

To get away from an austere fiancé who has given her emotional hangups, she comes to New York. She wants to turn professional, and asks Tracy to be her trainer and manager. He is astonished to hear that she is also proficient in tennis, swimming, and basketball. "There's a chance you could be an escaped fruitcake," he tells her incredulously. He soon finds that she is telling the truth and puts her through rigid training. She loses a tennis match only because her jinx of a fiancé reappears to unsettle her nerves. Hepburn ultimately decides that the unlikely Tracy would make a better husband for her, but she has to use persuasion. He can't understand why a high-class dame would want "my kind of type that can't even speak left-handed English." In the end, they achieve both personal happiness and fame in the sports world. "What would you ever do without me?" she asks. "I'd go right down the drain and take you with me, Shorty," is his reply.°

In addition to an abundance of amusing comedy situations, Tracy and Hepburn are given the opportunity to play four near-love scenes with finesse as their relationship gradually develops.

Not too much can be said for *Plymouth Adventure* (1952), Tracy's first color film in over a dozen years. This elaborate MGM production was based on Ernest Gebler's historical novel about the Pilgrims' long and hazardous sea voyage to Plymouth Rock on the *Mayflower*. Tracy had an unsympathetic part as the captain in charge of the journey, who despises his passengers. He also tries to seduce a married woman (Gene Tierney) and is indirectly responsible for her death from drowning. The tragedy chastens him and he helps the colony survive in the New World.

The veteran Clarence Brown

°Tracy also had a much-quoted line about Hepburn. Ogling her with satisfaction, he remarks: "She hasn't got much meat on her, but what she's got is *cherce*!"

THE ACTRESS (1953). With Jean Simmons and Teresa Wright

THE ACTRESS (1953). With Jean Simmons and Teresa Wright

directed a good cast that included Van Johnson, Leo Genn, and Lloyd Bridges. But Tracy hated his role and the overly contrived fictional plot.

He was much happier with *The Actress*, 1953), which George Cukor directed from Ruth Gordon's adaptation of her autobiographical play *Years Ago*. *The Actress* recounts Miss Gordon's girlhood and family life in pre-World War I New England. On the stage, her parents were enacted by Fredric March and Florence Eldridge. Tracy and Teresa Wright played these parts in the screen version, with the young British actress Jean Simmons in the title role: Anthony Perkins appeared as her shy suitor.

Tracy contributed one of his most endearing characterizations as a gruff but lovable ex-sea captain. He first tries to discourage his daughter's theatrical aspirations, but then allows her to go to New York with his blessings. Tracy's best scene involved his long description of his hard boyhood. *The Actress* was not a financial success, but it remains a fine piece of Americana, full of gentle nostalgia and authentic period atmosphere.

After *The Actress*, Tracy did not make a film for over a year. He was impressed with Ernest Hemingway's Pulitzer Prize-winning short novel *The Old Man and the Sea*, but MGM showed no interest in it. When independent producer Leland Hayward obtained the rights, Tracy agreed to star in it at some future date.

His present MGM contract allowed for outside pictures, and he returned to 20th Century-Fox for the first time in fifteen years to star in *Broken Lance* (1954). This top-budgeted Cinemascope color Western marked his first appearance in the new screen process. The picture, directed by Edward Dmytryk and filmed on location in Arizona, was reminiscent of *The Sea of Grass* in its storyline. It also borrowed liberally (with proper credit) from Philip Yordan's screenplay for *House of Strangers*, a non-Western which 20th Century-Fox had produced in 1949. A tale of intra-family tensions, *Broken Lance* cast Tracy as a lawless cattle baron hated by the sons of his first marriage and loved by the half-breed son (Robert Wagner) of his second. After Wagner takes responsibility for a raid led by Tracy and goes to prison, the other sons declare open rebellion against Tracy and the shock kills him. The role was a physically strenuous one for the now white-haired Tracy, but he managed the dangerous horseback riding scenes and enjoyed doing the

BROKEN LANCE (1954). As Matt Devereaux

film.

Bad Day at Black Rock was the last picture Tracy made for MGM with the exception of *How the West Was Won* (1963), for which the actor supplied the narration. He did not want to do *Bad Day*, and Dore Schary had to talk him into it. Tracy changed his mind about the picture during the sweltering location filming near Death Valley in the summer of 1954. The picture was shaping up so well under John Sturges's direction that he felt it was going to be worth all the discomfort. And he was right. The film, one of the best in 1955, gave Tracy his finest dramatic opportunity in years and also earned him a fifth Oscar nomination.

Bad Day at Black Rock is both a suspense thriller and a mystery story, and mounting tension is admirably sustained throughout the film. The entire action takes place during one day and night. The time is late 1945.

A feeling of excitement is established from the very first shots of a speeding train during the opening credits. The train stops at a desolate desert town and a one-armed man (Tracy) gets off. Two mean-looking men (Lee Marvin and Ernest Borgnine) regard him suspiciously. His manner is mysterious, and they are menacing in their speech. "I'll only be here twenty-four hours" is all that he will tell them. Tracy walks through the town. The few inhabitants he finds to talk to are either unfriendly or outwardly hostile. He wants to go to nearby Adobe Flats, but no one will drive him there.

Eventually we learn the stranger's mission. He has come to present a Japanese-American soldier's posthumous medal to the dead man's father. But the father had been brutally murdered four years earlier by some of the town's prejudice-crazed men led by Robert Ryan. They try to frighten Tracy out of town with threats of violence before he can discover the truth. In a final bloody showdown, he thwarts his oppressors with the help of a Molotov cocktail.

Tracy portrayed the strong, silent man of action to perfection in this gripping film, marred only by the wildly improbable melodramatics at the end.

MGM next scheduled *Tribute to a Bad Man* for the star. It was another Western and Tracy balked at the assignment. He considered the script inferior to *Broken Lance* and he did not feel up to another arduous location trek. Once again, he was persuaded to make a film against

BAD DAY AT BLACK ROCK (1955). With Lee Marvin

BAD DAY AT BLACK ROCK (1955). With Robert Ryan

his better judgment.

In June 1955 location work began, under Robert Wise's direction, in the Rocky Mountains near Montrose, California. Tracy arrived six days late without explanation. It was obvious to all that the actor was in an ugly mood. His subsequent behavior equaled anything he had done at Fox in the thirties. The day after his arrival, he disappeared and could not be found anywhere. Wise shot around him until there was nothing else to film. Production had to be shut down. Director, cast, and crew—some one hundred forty people—just sat there, hoping for Tracy's return. The delay cost MGM thirty thousand dollars a day. Tracy suddenly reappeared a week later. Again no explanation, but he said he was ready to begin work. He did a few scenes and completely ignored Wise's instructions. Wise was furious at what he considered Tracy's attempt to take over the production. Tracy worked three half days. He would always quit just before lunchtime, and refused to return in the afternoon. Finally, Tracy made an impossible demand. He wanted an expensive ranch set moved from an eight-thousand foot elevation to a site two thousand feet lower. He said he could not stand the altitude. Wise explained that relocating the set would cause a three-month delay. Tracy still insisted, and Wise fired him. Tracy was replaced by James Cagney.

Tracy's reasons for his actions have never been made public. He and MGM parted company after an association of twenty years. It was a sad occasion for both the actor and the studio, but a reasonably amicable one in view of the circumstances. Tracy even received a pension.

Firmly established as a super-star, the fifty-five-year old Tracy became a free-lance player. He could command three hundred thousand dollars a picture plus a percentage of the gross. He turned down all television offers until David Wolper persuaded him to host a series of six shows on American history. But the producer could not interest any of the major networks in the project, and the series was abandoned. Tracy never did appear on television.

He now spent most of his spare time with Katharine Hepburn and her circle of friends. He continued to see his family regularly, but refused to discuss any part of his personal life with the press. In fact, he discouraged all interviews. He had become a very private person.

One source of pride and satisfaction for Tracy was his two children's achievements. John had graduated from college and was working as an artist for Walt Disney. John married, and, in 1953, had a son whose hearing is normal. Tracy's daughter Susie, a talented musician, was studying voice.

Tracy found a story that he liked called *The Mountain*, and he and director Edward Dmytryk persuaded Paramount to finance and distribute the production.

THE FINAL YEARS (1956-1967)

The plot, set in the French Alps, concerned two brothers. Tracy, the eldest, had been a professional mountain climber, now long retired. The picture was filmed on location near Chamonix, France, in color and Vista-Vision. The company spent three months there. Tracy's role required much physical work and he later regretted the experience. But he could not complain about it to anyone since the venture was entirely his own idea.

Tracy was not too happily cast in this modern variation of the Cain and Abel legend, and Robert Wagner was not a very convincing younger brother. Tracy is a simple man of honor, while Wagner is totally dishonest. Wagner decides to climb Mont Blanc in order to plunder the wreckage of a plane crash. Tracy, fearing the dangers involved, makes the perilous ascent with him. When they reach their destination, Tracy rescues the plane's sole survivor (Anna Kashfi), and sees his brother fall to his death.

The Mountain was an expensive picture that failed to

THE MOUNTAIN (1956). With Robert Wagner

generate much excitement. It received an indifferent reception from both critics and public.

Undaunted, Tracy was willing to attempt another location trek. Producer Leland Hayward had obtained backing for *The Old Man and the Sea* from Warner Brothers. In the summer of 1956, the film began production in Cuba with Tracy as star. It was a major undertaking which received a vast amount of press coverage, since the Hemingway novella had achieved the status of a modern American classic. There were many production problems, due to poor weather conditions and a dispute between Hayward and director Fred Zinnemann over the script. The film was way behind sched-

ule when Zinnemann quit. Further bad weather forced Hayward to halt production. A decision was made to resume work at the Warner studio in Burbank using an artificial ocean containing seven hundred and fifty thousand gallons of water. It would take considerable time to make the necessary preparations, and the shutdown left Tracy free to accept an interim picture.

Hepburn persuaded him to appear with her in *The Desk Set* (1957), a comedy adapted from a recent Broadway hit, which 20th Century-Fox was producing. His part was built up from the original and completely altered to make it a romantic lead. And it was the last time Tracy played

THE DESK SET (1957). With Katharine Hepburn

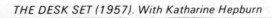

THE DESK SET (1957). With Katharine Hepburn

THE OLD MAN AND THE SEA (1958). As the Old Man

such a role. Twentieth Century-Fox gave it a handsome production and smooth direction by Walter Lang. The result: a mild but agreeable light farce, certainly the better for Tracy and Hepburn's charming performances.

The Desk Set is a reworking of the familiar battle-of-the-sexes formula in a modern setting. Hepburn played the head of a television network's reference and research department who matches wits with a stern efficiency expert (Tracy), hired to replace her girls with an electronic brain. As usual, opposites attract and antagonism turns to love. The slender storyline is so deftly handled and the acting so sprightly that the film's lack of substance passes unnoticed.

Tracy went out to Warners' Burbank studios to resume work on *The Old Man and the Sea.* The story of this modern parable is simplicity itself. Tracy portrayed a poor Cuban fisherman who has not caught a fish in months. His luck changes and he succeeds in catching a huge marlin only to see it devoured by sharks before he can bring it to shore.

During the long shooting schedule, Tracy lost his enthusiasm for the picture. He doubted that so much footage of a solitary man in a little boat could hold the attention of audiences. The final version had Tracy on screen alone for an hour of the film's eighty-six minutes. He also spoke the off-screen narration. Curiously, he did not attempt a Spanish accent for the role.

THE OLD MAN AND THE SEA (1958). As the Old Man

When the film was completed after almost two years in production, it was estimated that costs had soared to six million dollars. Tracy reportedly owned a one-third interest in it, but he didn't realize much money from the venture. The picture was a commercial failure and reviews were mixed, although many critics had kind things to say about Tracy's performance, which received an Academy Award nomination.

The Old Man and the Sea had been a long and strenuous ordeal for Tracy and a very disappointing experience. John Ford, who had directed Tracy's first picture, offered him a role that proved to be just the tonic he needed—the lead in *The Last Hurrah*, based on Edwin O'Connor's best selling novel. Ford surrounded Tracy with an exceptionally fine supporting cast of veteran actors including Pat O'Brien, Basil Rathbone, Donald Crisp, John Carradine, James Gleason, and Edward Brophy who was especially wonderful as the foolish, devoted Ditto.

The Last Hurrah derives its inspiration from the life and times of Boston's Mayor James M. Curley. Tracy portrayed Frank Skeffington, a genial Irish-American political boss who is mayor of an unspecified New England city. He has a coterie of loyal admirers and is loved by much of the populace, but he also has his share of enemies. These include a powerful newspaper publisher (John Carradine). He has a worthless son, but he remains faithful to the memory of his wife by placing a rose under her portrait each day.

Frank stages his "last hurrah"—his fifth and final campaign for mayoralty. He is the popular candidate and sure to win. But unexpectedly he loses. "I'm sorry the show didn't have a happier ending," he tells his staff. "Maybe I can do better the next time."

Frank announces he'll run for governor next, but a heart attack soon puts an end to his career. He collapses on the stairway of his home after he leaves campaign headquarters. "I want to see my old friends," he tells the doctor on his deathbed. In a long but moving scene, they all come to pay their respects. He expires with friends, relatives, and even one adversary—his nephew's father-in-law—in attendance. "If he had his life to live over again, he probably would live it quite differently," remarks the adversary. Then Frank opens his eyes for one last rebuttal: "Like hell I would!"

Tracy relished his rich, fla-

THE LAST HURRAH (1958). With Jeffrey Hunter

THE LAST HURRAH (1958). With Ricardo Cortez and Pat O'Brien

vorsome role, and came through with a brilliant performance that ranks with his best work. Ford filled the picture with many memorable vignettes: Skeffington's confrontation of the bankers in their private club; a rowdy wake at which the none-too-beloved deceased is extolled ("A lovable man. His friends were legend"); Skeffington's clever ruse to disconcert his enemy Norman Kass (Basil Rathbone), and others.

In 1960, Tracy began his association with producer-director Stanley Kramer, which he regarded as one of the most rewarding of his career. He was teamed with Fredric March, another perennial actor's actor, in *Inherit the Wind,* the screen version of the Jerome Lawrence-Robert E. Lee stage play, based on the notorious 1925 Scopes monkey trial in Dayton, Tennessee. Tracy and March played the prototypes of Clarence Darrow and William Jennings Bryan, the defender and prosecutor respectively of a young high-school biology teacher accused of teaching Darwin's theory of evolution in defiance of Tennessee law.

Filmed in crisp black-and-white, it was one of the year's important films and Tracy's impersonation of Darrow, renamed Henry Drummond, won him still another Oscar nomination. Most of the action takes place in the hot, stuffy courtroom, and throughout the filming the two stars engaged in friendly competition trying to excel each other in the display of their individual acting styles. March, strutting like a peacock, gave a showy, flamboyant interpretation of the smug, self-righteous ex-Presidential candidate, while Tracy held himself in and achieved his effects by allowing his character to build slowly and steadily increase in momentum. One critic called it the acting battle of the year.

Tracy gave a thoughtful and touching performance in *The Devil at Four O'Clock* (1961), costarring with Frank Sinatra. Tracy portrayed an aging, alcoholic priest on a small French island in the South Pacific who is being relieved of his duties by a younger priest. Partially filmed on location in Hawaii, the movie, an adventure story rooted in character rather than simple action, derives its title from an old saying: "It's hard for a man to be brave when he knows he is going to meet the devil at four o'clock."

In the film, Tracy is regarded as something of a curiosity by the villagers. He is seedy in appearance and seemingly eccentric in manner. He is always beg-

INHERIT THE WIND (1960). With Fredric March

INHERIT THE WIND (1960). With Donna Anderson

ging money and small gifts for an isolated leper hospital in the mountains. Most of the patients are children and Tracy spends much of his time there. He is soon revealed as a man of great courage and integrity.

His first meeting with Sinatra, one of three convicts, occurs after the men have arrived on the island and are about to be put in solitary confinement. He wants the men to help him at the hospital and can get permission to have them put in his charge. Sinatra is unwilling to go. "When I was a kid in Hell's Kitchen, we used to eat punks like you," Tracy tells him. Sinatra's reply: "That was when you had your teeth." The prisoners decide that working at the hospital is better than being in jail, and agree to help. Sinatra eventually falls in love with a blind native nurse.

The young priest who is taking over Tracy's duties learns from a doctor why the older man turned to drink. Tracy was a dedicated man who came to the island to build the hospital in the community. The town turned against him because the citizens didn't want a leper hospital that would kill tourism. It had to be constructed in the mountains. "I had to watch a good man crumble and open up at the seams," the doctor says.

THE DEVIL AT FOUR O'CLOCK (1961). With native children

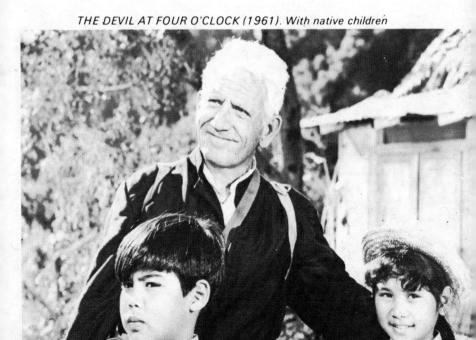

JUDGMENT AT NUREMBERG (1961). As Judge Dan Haywood

JUDGMENT AT NUREMBERG (1961). With Marlene Dietrich

Tracy is able to perform one last heroic act that costs him his life. With the help of the three convicts, he sees that the patients and staff of the hospital reach safety during a volcanic eruption.

The volcanic eruption and earthquake scenes are well done, and the perilous descent down the mountains is an exciting sequence. *The Devil at Four O'Clock* is an interesting movie that just missed the mark as completely satisfying screen entertainment.

Tracy's second film for Kramer, released almost simultaneously with *The Devil at Four O'Clock* in 1961, was the ambitious *Judgment at Nuremberg*. The picture, which scriptwriter Abby Mann expanded from his television play, had an impressive all-star cast in addition to Tracy. It included Burt Lancaster, Richard Widmark, Marlene Dietrich, Montgomery Clift, and Judy Garland. Tracy received his eighth Academy Award nomination for this picture, but lost out to Maximilian Schell, who won the Oscar for his role in the film.

Tracy was most enthusiastic about the three-hour production, which required extensive location work in Berlin. He considered the script one of the best he had ever read. He played a re-tired US judge assigned in 1948 to head a tribunal in Germany against four Nazis accused of perpetrating atrocities during Hitler's regime. Lancaster was a grim and rigid defendant who finally acknowledges his guilt, Schell the forceful defense attorney, Widmark the chief prosecutor, and Clift and Garland, in relatively small roles, appeared as two pathetic witnesses. Marlene Dietrich had an incidental part, that of a high-born German widow who befriends Tracy in his off-duty hours.

Judgment at Nuremberg was a powerful and intelligently written film that raised many disturbing questions about guilt, responsibility, and vengeance. Kramer's skilled direction and the superb acting made the long courtroom scenes continuously absorbing. Tracy's judge was a strong, compassionate, realistic figure who has his own doubts about the trial and makes an effort in his spare time to probe the minds of the German people. His finest moment in the picture is his fourteen-minute summation of the trial at the film's end.

Tracy was now living in a little cottage on George Cukor's estate, which he rented from the director. Cukor and Stanley Kramer had become two of his closest friends, and Kramer

IT'S A MAD, MAD, MAD, MAD WORLD (1963). With William Demarest

seemed to be the only one offering Tracy roles that he wanted to do. Also, Tracy was beginning to suffer from increasing ill health.

He agreed to appear in Kramer's *It's a Mad, Mad, Mad, Mad World* (1963), a wild, wacky, marathon comedy, in Cinerama and color, that ran over three hours and was given a spectacular production. This grandiose mixture of slapstick farce and chase film was spun at a frenetic pace. The picture employed a huge cast of comedians and well-known names appeared even in tiny roles. Tracy played a crafty police captain observing the progress of various money-mad citizens out to beat each other in discovering the hiding place of three hundred and fifty

thousand stolen dollars. When discovery is at hand, Tracy moves in and decides he'd like to keep the money for himself. Cinerama cameras caught the sweep and excitement of racing cars and airplanes against beautiful California scenery, and the film has many hilarious scenes. But it was too top-heavy for the slender story it had to tell.

Tracy, looking aged and unwell, did, however, make the most of his sardonic role, which was one of the film's more important parts.

Kramer, aware that Tracy was ill, allowed the actor to work only a few hours a day, and saw to it that he was not in any of the Mojave Desert location scenes. It was reported that he was suffering from diabetes. But later his condition proved far more serious.

In June 1963 Tracy called for Katharine Hepburn at her Malibu Beach house. Before they could start on a picnic, he collapsed. Hepburn, fearing a heart attack, summoned the local fire company to administer oxygen. Tracy was rushed to a hospital in an ambulance. He remained there for two weeks. The attack, first diagnosed as "a little congestion in the lungs that embarrassed the heart," was later attributed to emphysema. When he returned home, a Hungarian couple employed by Cukor looked after him and Miss Hepburn rented a home nearby.

In December 1963 John Ford offered Tracy a role in *Cheyenne Autumn*, which he accepted. But he was too ill to report to work when filming began on location. Ford revised the script in the hope that Tracy might be able to do his scenes in a studio. Tracy's doctor advised against it, and Edward G. Robinson replaced him in the picture.

In 1964, Tracy's health improved and he agreed to play the old gambler who pits his skill against a younger man in *The Cincinnati Kid*. Before start of production at MGM, he suffered a relapse. Once again, Edward G. Robinson took over the role for Tracy.

For the first eight months of 1965, Tracy lived in seclusion and practically never left his home. In early September of that year, he went back to the hospital for the removal of his prostate. There were complications and for twenty-four hours he was close to death. Mrs. Tracy and Hepburn kept a continual bedside vigil by turns. Tracy slowly recovered and, at the end of the month, he was allowed to go home.

Nothing about Tracy appeared in print for a year. Then, in October 1966, Kramer announced that Tracy and Hepburn would costar with Sidney Poitier in *Guess Who's Coming to Dinner*. Hepburn herself had not made a picture in four years. She had retired temporarily from the screen to devote all her time to Tracy.

Hollywood received the news of Tracy's return to the screen with skepticism. People believed that Tracy was dying and that he would never be able to start the picture. Kramer could not get insurance companies to cover Tracy, but the actor was so eager to do one more picture that Kramer decided to go ahead anyway.

Both Tracy and Hepburn

GUESS WHO'S COMING TO DINNER (1967). With Katharine Hepburn

liked the William Rose script, which would serve to introduce Katharine Houghton, Miss Hepburn's niece, to the screen as their daughter. Production started on February 19, 1967. Throughout filming, there was much apprehension as to whether Tracy would be able to complete the picture. But with Hepburn · and Kramer's help, Tracy managed to pull through.

Tracy looks worn and lined in the movie, but he walks with sureness and projects much of his old vigor. There is only an occasional crack and quiver in his voice, which the actor valiantly tries to hide. At no time does the audience get the feeling that they are watching a dying man. He is in complete command of his role and contributes an eloquent and assured performance.

Guess Who's Coming to Dinner tackled a serious subject— racial intermarriage—and treated it lightly but with deftness, charm, and a gentle touch of humor. It is presented in the straightforward manner of a stage play, with most of the important dialogue scenes taking place on one set.

A young girl (Houghton) brings her black fiancé (Poitier) home to San Francisco to meet her family. They met on a Hawaiian vacation and have known each other only a few weeks. He is a brilliant doctor and she is the daughter of liberal, well-to-do parents. The father (Tracy) is a newspaper publisher, and the mother (Hepburn) runs a modern art gallery. The girl wants to marry immediately, but the doctor has grave doubts.

The family knows nothing about it. Hepburn is the first to receive the news. She is flabbergasted, but tries to make the doctor feel welcome. Then Tracy comes home for lunch. "Do you want an answer today about how your mother and I feel?" he asks, remaining outwardly calm. Poitier then tells Tracy that the marriage will not take place without his approval.

Alone, Tracy and Hepburn discuss the problem.

Tracy: "Did it ever occur to you that this might happen? They may know what they're saying, but they don't know what they're doing."

Hepburn: "We brought our daughter up to believe all people are equal. But when we said it, we did not add 'don't fall in love with a colored man.' "

Later Tracy asks Poitier: "Have you given any thought to the children you are going to have? No matter how confident you two are, I'm just a little scared."

Hepburn then invites the doctor's parents to fly up from Los Angeles for dinner. They are just as deeply concerned as Tracy and Hepburn, and try earnestly to express their feelings about a difficult situation. The mothers are sympathetic, but the two fathers agree that the marriage would be a grave mistake.

Troubled and angry, the doctor's mother (Beah Richards) tells Tracy bluntly that he doesn't know how it feels to be in love; Tracy meditates alone in the garden and ponders her words. "Well, I'll be a son of a bitch!" he says as he comes to a sudden realization. Finally, he goes in to face the assembled principals and delivers a moving speech.

"It's been a very strange, an extraordinary day," he begins. "My daughter informed me that she intended to marry a Negro, and that the marriage would take place no matter how I felt. My wife is in a romantic haze inaccessible to reason. I've been

141

GUESS WHO'S COMING TO DINNER (1967). With Katharine Hepburn

called a burnt-out shell of a man who can't remember what it is like to love a woman. You're wrong. I know exactly how he feels about her. There is nothing, exactly nothing, that I don't remember about how I feel. If what they feel for each other is even half of what *we* felt [looking at Hepburn]—then that is everything."

Tracy's talk convinces everyone that the marriage should take place.

Tracy was elated when the picture was completed on May 26, 1967. He frankly didn't think he was going to make it. He retired immediately to his cottage "very happy and very tired." According to George Cukor, he just wanted to rest.

142

Two weeks later he was dead. Death came to him on June 10, 1967, just before 6:00 A.M. Heart failure was given as the official cause. Although everyone had been expecting it, his passing was a great shock and millions throughout the world mourned him.

Guess Who's Coming to Dinner received nine Academy Award nominations the following year, including a posthumous one for Tracy. He lost out to Rod Steiger. Hepburn, a dark horse, surprisingly won for Best Actress. When she expressed her thanks, she said she considered it a joint award for both herself and Spencer Tracy.

He was gone, but for more than thirty-five years, his strong presence, his unwavering honesty, his special blending of warmth, humor, and toughness had pleased film audiences. An indisputable member of the select group of enduring film actors, he would be long remembered.

143

THE FILMS OF SPENCER TRACY

The director's name follows the release date. A (c) following the release date indicates that the film was in color. Sp indicates screenplay and b/o indicates based/on.

1. UP THE RIVER. Fox, 1930. *John Ford.* Sp: Maurine Watkins, b/o her story. Cast: Claire Luce, Warren Hymer, Humphrey Bogart, Joan Marie Lawes, William Collier, Sr. Remade in 1938.

2. QUICK MILLIONS. Fox, 1931. *Rowland Brown.* Sp: Courtney Terrett & Rowland Brown, b/o their story. Cast: Sally Eilers, Marguerite Churchill, John Wray, George Raft, Bob Burns, Warner Richmond.

3. SIX CYLINDER LOVE. Fox, 1931. *Thornton Freeland.* Sp: William Conselman & Norman Houston, b/o play by William 'Anthony McGuire. Cast: Sidney Fox, Edward Everett Horton, William Collier, Sr., Una Merkel, Lorin Raker, Bert Roach, El Brendel.

4. GOLDIE. Fox, 1931. *Benjamin Stoloff.* Sp: Gene Towne & Paul Perez, b/o story by Howard Hawks & James K. McGuinness. Cast: Warren Hymer, Jean Harlow, Lina Basquette, Eleanor Hunt, Maria Alba, ·Eddie Kane. Remake of Howard Hawks's 1928 Fox silent *A Girl in Every Port.*

5. SHE WANTED A MILLIONAIRE. Fox, 1932. *John G. Blystone.* Sp: William Anthony McGuire, b/o story by Sonya Levien. Cast: Joan Bennett, Una Merkel, James Kirkwood, Dorothy Peterson, Donald Dillaway.

6. SKY DEVILS. United Artists, 1932. *Edward Sutherland.* Sp: Joseph Moncure March & Edward Sutherland, b/o their story. Cast: Ann Dvorak, William Boyd, George Cooper, Billy Bevan, Yola D'Avril.

7. DISORDERLY CONDUCT. Fox, 1932. *John W. Considine, Jr.* Sp: William Anthony McGuire, b/o his story. Cast: Sally Eilers, El Brendel, Dickie Moore, Ralph Bellamy, Ralph Morgan, Alan Dinehart, Charles Grapewin, Sally Blane.

8. YOUNG AMERICA. Fox, 1932. *Frank Borzage.* Sp: William Conselman, b/o play by John Frederick Ballard. Cast: Doris Kenyon, Tommy Conlon, Ralph Bellamy, Raymond Borzage, Sarah Padden, Beryl Mercer, Dawn O'Day (Anne Shirley). First filmed by Essanay in 1922.

9. SOCIETY GIRL. Fox, 1932. *Sidney Lanfield*. Sp: Elmer Harris, b/o play by John Larkin, and Charles Beahan Jr. Cast: James Dunn, Peggy Shannon, Walter Byron, Marjorie Gateson.

10. THE PAINTED WOMAN. Fox, 1932. *John G. Blystone*. Sp: Guy Bolton & Leon Gordon, b/o play by Alfred C. Kennedy & story by Larry Evans. Cast: Peggy Shannon, William Boyd, Irving Pichel, Raul Roulien, Murray Kinnell. Remake of 1924 Fox silent *The Painted Lady*.

11. ME AND MY GAL. Fox, 1932. *Raoul Walsh*. Sp: Arthur Kober, b/o story by Barry Conners and Philip Klein. Cast: Joan Bennett, Marion Burns, George Walsh, J. Farrell MacDonald, Henry B. Walthall. Remade by Fox in 1940 as *Pier 13*.

12. 20,000 YEARS IN SING SING. First National, 1933. *Michael Curtiz*. Sp: Courtney Territt, Robert Lord, Wilson Mizner and Brown Holmes, b/o book by Lewis E. Lawes. Cast: Bette Davis, Lyle Talbot, Louis Calhern, Sheila Terry, Warren Hymer, Arthur Byron, Grant Mitchell. Remade by Warners in 1940 as *Castle on the Hudson*.

13. FACE IN THE SKY. Fox, 1933. *Harry Lachman*. Sp: Humphrey Pearson, b/o story by Myles Connolly. Cast: Marian Nixon, Stuart Erwin, Lila Lee, Sam Hardy, Russell Simpson, Sarah Padden.

14. THE POWER AND THE GLORY. Fox, 1933. *William K. Howard*. Sp: Preston Sturges, b/o his story. Cast: Colleen Moore, Ralph Morgan, Helen Vinson, Clifford Jones, Henry Kolker, Sarah Padden.

15. SHANGHAI MADNESS. Fox, 1933. *John G. Blystone*. Sp: Austin Parker, b/o story by Frederick Hazlitt Brennan. Cast: Fay Wray, Ralph Morgan, Eugene Pallette, Herbert Mundin, Reginald Mason.

16. THE MAD GAME. Fox, 1933. *Irving Cummings*. Sp: William Conselman and Henry Johnson, b/o their story. Cast: Claire Trevor, Ralph Morgan, J. Carrol Naish, John Miljan, Mary Mason, Howard Lally.

17. MAN'S CASTLE. Columbia, 1933. *Frank Borzage*. Sp: Jo Swerling, b/o play by Lawrence Hazard. Cast: Loretta Young, Glenda Farrell, Walter Connolly, Marjorie Rambeau, Arthur Hohl.

18. LOOKING FOR TROUBLE. 20th Century-United Artists, 1934. *William A. Wellman*. Sp: Leonard Praskins and Elmer Harris, b/o story by J. R. Bren. Cast: Jack Oakie, Constance Cummings, Arline Judge, Judith Wood, Morgan Conway, Paul Harvey.

19. THE SHOW-OFF. MGM, 1934. *Charles F. Reisner*. Sp: Herman J. Mankiewicz, b/o play by George Kelly. Cast: Madge Evans, Lois Wilson, Grant Mitchell, Clara Blandick, Claude Gillingwater, Henry Wadsworth. Previously filmed in 1926 and 1930. Also remade by MGM in 1947.

20. BOTTOMS UP. Fox, 1934. *David Butler*. Sp: B. G. DeSylva, David Butler and Sid Silvers, b/o their story. Cast: John Boles, Pat Paterson, Herbert Mundin, Thelma Todd, Sid Silvers, Harry Green.

21. NOW I'LL TELL. Fox, 1934. *Edwin Burke*. Sp: Edwin Burke, b/o book by Mrs. Arnold Rothstein. Cast: Helen Twelvetrees, Alice Faye, Robert Gleckler, Hobart Cavanaugh, Henry O'Neill, Shirley Temple.

22. MARIE GALANTE. Fox, 1934. *Henry King*. Sp: Reginald Berkeley, b/o play by Jacques Deval. Cast: Ketti Gallian, Ned Sparks, Helen Morgan, Sig Rumann, Leslie Fenton, Arthur Byron, Stepin Fetchit.

23. IT'S A SMALL WORLD. Fox, 1935. *Irving Cummings*. Sp: Sam Hellman and Gladys Lehman, b/o story by Albert Treynor. Cast: Wendy Barrie, Raymond Walburn, Virginia Sale, Astrid Allwyn, Charles Sellon, Nick (Dick) Foran.

24. MURDER MAN. MGM, 1935. *Tim Whelan*. Sp: Tim Whelan and John C. Higgins, b/o story by Whelan and Guy Bolton. Cast: Virginia Bruce, Lionel Atwill, Harvey Stephens, Robert Barrat, James Stewart, William Demarest, William Collier, Sr.

25. DANTE'S INFERNO. Fox, 1935. *Harry Lachman*. Sp: Philip Klein and Robert M. Yost. Cast: Claire Trevor, Henry B. Walthall, Alan Dinehart, Scotty Beckett, Robert Gleckler, Rita Cansino (Hayworth).

26. WHIPSAW. MGM, 1935. *Sam Wood*. Sp: Howard E. Rogers, b/o story by James E. Grant. Cast: Myrna Loy, Harvey Stephens, William Harrigan, Clay Clement, Robert Gleckler, Robert Warwick.

27. RIFFRAFF. MGM, 1935. *J. Walter Ruben*. Sp: Frances Marion, H. W. Hanemann and Anita Loos, b/o story by Frances Marion. Cast: Jean Harlow, Una Merkel, Joseph Calleia, Victor Kilian, Mickey Rooney.

28. FURY. MGM, 1936. *Fritz Lang*. Sp: Bartlett Cormack and Fritz Lang, b/o story by Norman Krasna. Cast: Sylvia Sidney, Walter Abel, Bruce Cabot, Edward Ellis, Walter Brennan, Frank Albertson.

29. SAN FRANCISCO. MGM, 1936. *W. S. Van Dyke II*. Sp: Anita Loos, b/o story by Robert Hopkins. Cast: Clark Gable, Jeanette MacDonald, Jack Holt, Jessie Ralph, Ted Healy, Shirley Ross, Kenneth Harlan, Warren Hymer. ST's first Academy Award nomination.

30. LIBELED LADY. MGM, 1936. *Jack Conway*. Sp: Maurine Watkins, Howard Emmett Rogers and George Oppenheimer, b/o story by Wallace Sullivan. Cast: Jean Harlow, William Powell, Myrna Loy, Walter Connolly, Charles Grapewin, Cora Witherspoon. Remade by MGM in 1946 as *Easy to Wed*.

31. THEY GAVE HIM A GUN. MGM, 1937. *W. S. Van Dyke II*. Sp: Cyril Hume, Richard Maibaum and Maurice Rapf, b/o book by William Joyce Cowen. Cast: Gladys George, Franchot Tone, Edgar Dearing, Mary Lou (Mary) Treen, Cliff Edwards, Joan Woodbury.

32. CAPTAINS COURAGEOUS. MGM, 1937. *Victor Fleming*. Sp: John

Lee Mahin, Marc Connelly and Dale Van Every, b/o novel by Rudyard Kipling. Cast: Freddie Bartholomew, Lionel Barrymore, Melvyn Douglas, Charles Grapewin, Mickey Rooney, John Carradine. Tracy's first Oscar-winning performance.

33. BIG CITY, MGM, 1937. *Frank Borzage*. Sp: Dore Schary and Hugo Butler, b/o story by Norman Krasna. Cast: Luise Rainer, Charley Grapewin, Janet Beecher, Eddie Quillan, Victor Varconi, Oscar O'Shea, Helen Troy.

34. MANNEQUIN. MGM, 1938. *Frank Borzage*. Sp: Lawrence Hazard, b/o story by Katharine Brush. Cast: Joan Crawford, Alan Curtis, Ralph Morgan, Mary Phillips, Oscar O'Shea, Elizabeth Risdon, Leo Gorcey.

35. TEST PILOT. MGM, 1938. *Victor Fleming*. Sp: Vincent Lawrence and Waldemar Young, b/o story by Frank Wead. Cast: Clark Gable, Myrna Loy, Lionel Barrymore, Samuel S. Hinds, Marjorie Main, Ted Pearson, Gloria Holden, Virginia Grey.

36. BOYS TOWN. MGM, 1938. *Norman Taurog*. Sp: John Meehan and Dore Schary, b/o story by Dore Schary and Eleanore Griffin. Cast: Mickey Rooney, Henry Hull, Leslie Fenton, Addison Richards, Edward Norris, Gene Reynolds, Minor Watson, Victor Kilian, Bobs Watson. Tracy won his second Oscar.

37. STANLEY AND LIVINGSTONE. 20th Century-Fox, 1939. *Henry King*. Sp: Philip Dunne and Julien Josephson, b/o research material by Hal Long and Sam Hellman. Cast: Nancy Kelly, Richard Greene, Walter Brennan, Charles Coburn, Sir Cedric Hardwicke, Henry Hull, Henry Travers, Miles Mander, David Torrence.

38. I TAKE THIS WOMAN. MGM, 1940. *W. S. Van Dyke II*. Sp: James Kevin McGuinness, b/o story by Charles MacArthur. Cast: Hedy Lamarr, Verree Teasdale, Kent Taylor, Laraine Day, Mona Barrie, Jack Carson, Paul Cavanagh, Louis Calhern, Marjorie Main, Frances Drake.

39. NORTHWEST PASSAGE. MGM, 1940. (c) *King Vidor*. Sp: Laurence Stallings and Talbot Jennings, b/o novel by Kenneth Roberts. Cast: Robert Young, Walter Brennan, Ruth Hussey, Nat Pendleton, Louis Hector, Robert Barrat, Isabel Jewell, Lumsden Hare, Donald McBride, Regis Toomey, Douglas Walton, Montagu Love.

40. EDISON THE MAN. MGM, 1940. *Clarence Brown*. Sp: Talbot Jennings and Bradbury Foote, b/o story by Dore Schary and Hugo Butler. Cast: Rita Johnson, Lynne Overman, Charles Coburn, Gene Lockhart, Henry Travers, Felix Bressart.

41. BOOM TOWN. MGM, 1940. *Jack Conway*. Sp: John Lee Mahin, b/o story by James Edward Grant. Cast: Clark Gable, Claudette Colbert, Hedy Lamarr, Frank Morgan, Lionel Atwill, Chill Wills, Minna Gombell, Marion Martin.

42. MEN OF BOYS TOWN. MGM, 1941. *Norman Taurog*. Sp: James Kevin McGuinness, b/o his story. Cast: Mickey Rooney, Bobs Watson, Larry Nunn, Darryl Hickman, Henry O'Neill, Mary Nash, Lee J. Cobb, Addison Richards, Anne Revere.

43. DR. JEKYLL AND MR. HYDE. MGM, 1941. *Victor Fleming*. Sp: John Lee Mahin, b/o novel by Robert Louis Stevenson. Cast: Ingrid Bergman, Lana Turner, Donald Crisp, Barton MacLane, C. Aubrey Smith, Ian Hunter, Peter Godfrey, Sara Allgood. Previously filmed at least eight times, most notably with John Barrymore (1920) and Fredric March (1931).

44. WOMAN OF THE YEAR. MGM, 1942. *George Stevens*. Sp: Ring Lardner, Jr., and Michael Kanin, b/o their story. Cast: Katharine Hepburn, Fay Bainter, Reginald Owen, Minor Watson, William Bendix, Roscoe Karns, Sara Haden, Connie Gilchrist, Grant Withers. Remade by MGM in 1957 as *Designing Woman*.

45. TORTILLA FLAT. MGM, 1942. *Victor Fleming*. Sp: John Lee Mahin and Benjamin Glazer, b/o novel by John Steinbeck. Cast: Hedy Lamarr, John Garfield, Frank Morgan, Akim Tamiroff, Sheldon Leonard, John Qualen, Donald Meek, Connie Gilchrist, Allen Jenkins, Henry O'Neill.

46. KEEPER OF THE FLAME. MGM, 1942. *George Cukor*. Sp: Donald Ogden Stewart, b/o story by I. A. R. Wylie. Cast: Katharine Hepburn, Richard Whorf, Margaret Wycherly, Forrest Tucker, Frank Craven, Horace (Stephen) McNally, Audrey Christie, Darryl Hickman, Donald Meek, Percy Kilbride, Howard da Silva.

47. A GUY NAMED JOE. MGM, 1943. *Victor Fleming*. Sp: Dalton Trumbo, b/o story by Chandler Sprague and David Boehm. Cast: Irene Dunne, Van Johnson, Ward Bond, James Gleason, Lionel Barrymore, Barry Nelson, Don DeFore, Henry O'Neill, Esther Williams.

48. THE SEVENTH CROSS. MGM, 1944. *Fred Zinnemann*. Sp: Helen Deutsch, b/o book by Anna Seghers. Cast: Signe Hasso, Hume Cronyn, Jessica Tandy, Agnes Moorehead, Herbert Rudley, Ray Collins, Felix Bressart, George Macready, George Zucco.

49. THIRTY SECONDS OVER TOKYO. MGM, 1944. *Mervyn LeRoy*. Sp: Dalton Trumbo, b/o book by Ted W. Lawson and Robert Considine. Cast: Van Johnson, Robert Walker, Phyllis Thaxter, Tim Murdock, Scott McKay, Don DeFore, Robert Mitchum, Gordon McDonald, Leon Ames.

50. WITHOUT LOVE. MGM, 1945. *Harold S. Bucquet*. Sp: Donald Ogden Stewart, b/o play by Philip Barry. Cast: Katharine Hepburn, Lucille Ball, Keenan Wynn, Carl Esmond, Patricia Morison, Felix Bressart, Gloria Grahame.

51. THE SEA OF GRASS. MGM, 1947. *Elia Kazan*. Sp: Marguerite Roberts and Vincent Lawrence, b/o novel by Conrad Richter. Cast: Katharine Hepburn, Melvyn Douglas, Phyllis Thaxter, Robert Walker, Edgar Buchanan, Harry Carey, Ruth Nelson, James Bell.

52. CASS TIMBERLANE. MGM, 1947. *George Sidney.* Sp: Donald Ogden Stewart and Sonya Levien, b/o novel by Sinclair Lewis. Cast: Lana Turner, Zachary Scott, Tom Drake, Mary Astor, Albert Dekker, Margaret Lindsay, Rose Hobart, John Litel, Mona Barrie, Selena Royle, Josephine Hutchinson, Cameron Mitchell.

53. STATE OF THE UNION. MGM, 1948. *Frank Capra.* Sp: Anthony Veiller and Myles Connolly, b/o play by Howard Lindsay and Russel Crouse. Cast: Katharine Hepburn, Van Johnson, Angela Lansbury, Adolphe Menjou, Lewis Stone, Howard Smith, Charles Dingle, Maidel Turner, Raymond Walburn, Margaret Hamilton.

54. EDWARD, MY SON. MGM, 1949. *George Cukor.* Sp: Donald Ogden Stewart, b/o play by Robert Morley and Noel Langley. Cast: Deborah Kerr, Ian Hunter, Leueen MacGrath, James Donald, Mervyn Johns, Felix Aylmer, Walter Fitzgerald.

55. ADAM'S RIB. MGM, 1949. *George Cukor.* Sp: Garson Kanin and Ruth Gordon, b/o their story. Cast: Katharine Hepburn, Judy Holliday, Tom Ewell, David Wayne, Jean Hagen, Hope Emerson.

56. MALAYA. MGM, 1950. *Richard Thorpe.* Sp: Frank Fenton, b/o story by Manchester Boddy. Cast: James Stewart, Valentina Cortese, Sydney Greenstreet, John Hodiak, Lionel Barrymore, Gilbert Roland, Roland Winters.

57. FATHER OF THE BRIDE. MGM, 1950. *Vincente Minnelli.* Sp: Albert Hackett and Frances Goodrich, b/o novel by Edward Streeter. Cast: Joan Bennett, Elizabeth Taylor, Don Taylor, Billie Burke, Leo G. Carroll, Moroni Olsen, Melville Cooper, Russ Tamblyn. Fourth Oscar nomination.

58. FATHER'S LITTLE DIVIDEND. MGM, 1951. *Vincente Minnelli.* Sp: Albert Hackett and Frances Goodrich, b/o characters created by Edward Streeter. Cast: Joan Bennett, Elizabeth Taylor, Don Taylor, Billie Burke, Moroni Olsen, Russ Tamblyn, Marietta Canty, Tom Irish.

59. THE PEOPLE AGAINST O'HARA. MGM, 1951. *John Sturges.* Sp: John Monks, Jr., b/o novel by Eleazar Lipsky. Cast: Diana Lynn, Pat O'Brien, John Hodiak, James Arness, Eduardo Ciannelli, Richard Anderson, Jay C. Flippen.

60. PAT AND MIKE. MGM, 1952. *George Cukor.* Sp: Ruth Gordon and Garson Kanin, b/o their story. Cast: Katharine Hepburn, Aldo Ray, William Ching, Sammy White, George Mathews, Phyllis Povah, Loring Smith.

61. PLYMOUTH ADVENTURE. MGM, 1952. (c) *Clarence Brown.* Sp: Helen Deutsch, b/o novel by Ernest Gebler. Cast: Gene Tierney, Van Johnson, Leo Genn, Lloyd Bridges, Dawn Addams, Barry Jones, Noel Drayton.

62. THE ACTRESS. MGM, 1953. *George Cukor.* Sp: Ruth Gordon, b/o her play *Years Ago.* Cast: Jean Simmons, Teresa Wright, Anthony Perkins, Ian Wolfe, Kay Williams, Mary Wickes, Norma Jean Nilsson, Dawn Bender.

63. BROKEN LANCE. 20th Century-Fox, 1954. (c) *Edward Dmytryk*. Sp: Richard Murphy, b/o story by Philip Yordan. Cast: Robert Wagner, Jean Peters, Richard Widmark, Katy Jurado, Hugh O'Brian, Eduard Franz, Earl Holliman, E. G. Marshall, Carl Benton Reid.

64. BAD DAY AT BLACK ROCK. MGM, 1955. (c) *John Sturges*. Sp: Millard Kaufman, b/o story by Howard Breslin. Cast: Robert Ryan, Anne Francis, Dean Jagger, Walter Brennan, John Ericson, Ernest Borgnine, Lee Marvin, Russell Collins, Walter Sande. Tracy's fifth Oscar-nominated performance.

65. THE MOUNTAIN. Paramount, 1956. (c) *Edward Dmytryk*. Sp: Ranald MacDougall, b/o novel by Henri Troyat. Cast: Robert Wagner, Claire Trevor, William Demarest, Barbara Darrow, E. G. Marshall, Anna Kashfi, Richard Arlen.

66. THE DESK SET. 20th Century-Fox, 1957. (c) *Walter Lang*. Sp: Phoebe and Henry Ephron, b/o play by William Marchant. Cast: Katharine Hepburn, Gig Young, Joan Blondell, Dina Merrill, Sue Randall, Neva Patterson.

67. THE OLD MAN AND THE SEA. Warner Brothers, 1958. (c) *John Sturges*. Sp: Peter Viertel, b/o novel by Ernest Hemingway. Cast: Felipe Pazos, Harry Bellaver. Tracy won his sixth Academy Award nomination.

68. THE LAST HURRAH. Columbia, 1958. *John Ford*. Sp: Frank Nugent, b/o novel by Edwin O'Connor. Cast: Jeffrey Hunter, Dianne Foster, Pat O'Brien, Basil Rathbone, Donald Crisp, James Gleason, Edward Brophy, John Carradine, Basil Ruysdael, Ricardo Cortez, Willis Bouchey, Wallace Ford, Frank McHugh, Anna Lee, Jane Darwell, Frank Albertson, Carleton Young.

69. INHERIT THE WIND. United Artists, 1960. *Stanley Kramer*. Sp: Nathan E. Douglas and Harold Jacob Smith, b/o play by Jerome Lawrence and Robert E. Lee. Cast: Fredric March, Gene Kelly, Florence Eldridge, Dick York, Donna Anderson, Harry Morgan, Elliott Reid, Noah Beery, Jr. Seventh Academy Award nomination for Tracy.

70. THE DEVIL AT FOUR O'CLOCK. Columbia, 1961. (c) *Mervyn LeRoy*. Sp: Liam O'Brien, b/o novel by Max Catto. Cast: Frank Sinatra, Kerwin Mathews, Jean Pierre Aumont, Gregoire Aslan, Alexander Scourby, Barbara Luna, Cathy Lewis.

71. JUDGMENT AT NUREMBERG. United Artists, 1961. *Stanley Kramer*. Sp: Abby Mann, b/o his TV play. Cast: Burt Lancaster, Richard Widmark, Marlene Dietrich, Maximilian Schell, Judy Garland, Montgomery Clift, Ed Binns, William Shatner, Kenneth MacKenna, Alan Baxter, Werner Klemperer, Torben Meyer, Virginia Christine, Ray Teal. Tracy's eighth Oscar nomination.

72. HOW THE WEST WAS WON. MGM, 1963. (c) *Henry Hathaway, John Ford, and George Marshall*. Sp: James R. Webb, b/o his story. Cast: Carroll Baker, Lee J. Cobb, Henry Fonda, Carolyn Jones, Karl Malden, Gregory

Peck, George Peppard, Robert Preston, Debbie Reynolds, James Stewart, Eli Wallach, John Wayne, Richard Widmark, Brigid Bazlen, Walter Brennan, David Brian, Andy Devine, Raymond Massey, Agnes Moorehead, Henry Morgan, Thelma Ritter.

73. IT'S A MAD, MAD, MAD, MAD WORLD. United Artists, 1963. (c) *Stanley Kramer*. Sp: William and Tania Rose, b/o their story. Cast: Milton Berle, Sid Caesar, Buddy Hackett, Ethel Merman, Mickey Rooney, Dick Shawn, Phil Silvers, Terry-Thomas, Jonathan Winters, Edie Adams, Jimmy Durante, Ben Blue, William Demarest, Peter Falk, Paul Ford, Edward Everett Horton, Buster Keaton.

74. GUESS WHO'S COMING TO DINNER. Columbia, 1967. (c) *Stanley Kramer*. Sp: William Rose, b/o his story. Cast: Sidney Poitier, Katharine Hepburn, Katharine Houghton, Cecil Kellaway, Beah Richards, Roy E. Glenn, Sr., Isabell Sanford, Virginia Christine. Tracy's ninth and last Academy Award-nominated performance.

THE SHORT FILMS OF SPENCER TRACY

1. TAXI TALKS. Warner Brothers-Vitaphone, 1930. *Arthur Hurley*. Cast: Vernon Wallace, Roger Pryor, Evalyn Knapp, Mayo Methot, Katherine Alexander. Two reels.

2. THE HARD GUY. Warner Brothers-Vitaphone, 1930. *Arthur Hurley*. Cast: Katherine Alexander.

3. RING OF STEEL. O. W. I., 1942. *Garson Kanin*. Sp: Kanin. A tribute to American soldiers from 1776 to 1942. Tracy spoke the narration. Produced by the Office of War Information's film unit. One reel.

4. BATTLE STATIONS. 20th Century-Fox, 1944. *Garson Kanin*. Sp: Kanin. Tracy and Ginger Rogers narrated this ten-minute short about Coast Guard Spars taking over shore jobs formerly filled by men.

5. TRAILER FOR THE AMERICAN CANCER SOCIETY, 1946. Tracy and Katharine Hepburn shared the narration.

6. TRAILER FOR THE TEXAS THEATERS CRIPPLED CHILDREN FUND, 1953. Tracy, as narrator, contributed importantly in raising one million dollars.

BIBLIOGRAPHY

Bennett, Joan and Kibbee, Lois. *The Bennett Playbill*. Holt, Rinehart and Winston, New York, 1970.

Capra, Frank. *The Name Above the Title*. The Macmillan Company, New York, 1971.

Descher, Donald. *The Films of Spencer Tracy*. The Citadel Press, New York, 1968.

Dickens, Homer. *The Films of Katharine Hepburn*. The Citadel Press, New York, 1971.

Kanin, Garson. *Tracy and Hepburn*. The Viking Press, Inc., New York, 1971.

Mantle, Burns. *The Best Plays of 1929-1930*. Dodd, Mead and Company, New York, 1930.

Swindell, Larry. *Spencer Tracy*. World Publishing Company, New York, 1969.

Vidor, King. *A Tree is a Tree*. Harcourt, Brace and Company, New York, 1953.

Articles

Ladies Home Journal: "Mrs. Spencer Tracy's Own Story" by Jane Ardmore, February 1973.

Look Magazine: "Spencer Tracy" by Bill Davidson, January 30, 1962.

The New York Daily News: "The Spencer Tracy Story" by Kitty Hanson, April 13-16, 1964.

INDEX

(Page numbers italicized indicate photographs)

155

158